EXPLORE YOUR POTENTIAL

A Journey through Eastern Mysticism

➤ *Use the Wisdom of Ancient Indian Texts*
➤ *Exercises to enhance intuitive perception*

Manish Vohra

Published by:

F-2/16, Ansari road, Daryaganj, New Delhi-110002
☎ 23240026, 23240027 • *Fax:* 011-23240028
Email: info@vspublishers.com • *Website:* www.vspublishers.com

Branch : Hyderabad
5-1-707/1, Brij Bhawan (Beside Central Bank of India Lane)
Bank Street, Koti Hyderabad - 500 095
☎ 040-24737290
E-mail: vspublishershyd@gmail.com

Distributors :

➤ **Pustak Mahal®**, Delhi
J-3/16, Daryaganj, New Delhi-110002
☎ 23276539, 23272783, 23272784 • *Fax:* 011-23260518
E-mail: sales@pustakmahal.com • *Website:* www.pustakmahal.com
Bengaluru: ☎ 080-22234025 • *Telefax:* 22240209
Patna: ☎ 0612-3294193 • *Telefax:* 0612-2302719

➤ **PM Publications**
- 10-B, Netaji Subhash Marg, Daryaganj, New Delhi-110002
  ☎ 23268292, 23268293, 23279900 • *Fax:* 011-23280567
  E-mail: rapidexdelhi@indiatimes.com, pmpublications@gmail.com
- 6686, Khari Baoli, Delhi-110006
  ☎ 23944314, 23911979

➤ **Unicorn Books**
Mumbai :
23-25, Zaoba Wadi (Opp. VIP Showroom), Thakurdwar, Mumbai-400002
☎ 22010941 • *Telefax:* 022-22053387

© Copyright: **V&S PUBLISHERS**
ISBN 978-93-813840-9-1
Edition: 2011

The Copyright of this book, as well as all matter contained herein (including illustrations) rests with the Publishers. No person shall copy the name of the book, its title design, matter and illustrations in any form and in any language, totally or partially or in any distorted form. Anybody doing so shall face legal action and will be responsible for damages.

Printed at : Param Offset, Okhla

Dedication

I would like to thank respected Sage Chandra Swamiji and Swami Prem Vivekanandji under whose guidance this book was written.

I would like to thank my parents and my brother from whom I learned the power of virtue and good intentions.

I would like to thank my beloved wife for her constant love and support and my children without whom my life would not be complete.

I would like to thank Mr. Sahil Gupta and the team at V&S Publishers for their constant support.

This book is dedicated with respect, love and gratitude to all beings. I would like to offer my salutation to all the sages who emanate unconditional love for all beings.

Salutation to Mother divine

MOTHER! IN PRAISE OF YOU
OH MOTHER......
ACCEPT THIS HYMN TO YOU
IN PRAISE OF YOU USING YOUR
OWN WORDS

Oh mother of all words!
This praise to you with your own words,
Is like giving to the Ocean
Its own water in offering.

Is like giving in offering to the moon
The little water of the moonstone.

Is like giving in offering to the sun
The flames of a lamp.

- Soundarya Lahari

Blessings of Respected Sage Shri. Chandra Swamiji

My hearty good wishes for Shri Manish Vohraji, for whom divine Love is the only thing worthy of attainment. May he be drawn closer and closer to God and be bathed in His Love and Light which alone dispels all doubts and darkness forever.

– **Chandra Swamiji Udasin**
Sadhana Kendra Ashram
Domet, Dehradun

Foreword

For Shri Manish Vohraji, the author of this book, the words contained within these pages are expressions of his love for the divine, which to him is the loftiest of all the ideals to be attained. He writes beautifully in the book, "This universe spins on love and surrender to God". In pursuit of his holy quest, he also attempts to understand and explain the great cosmic principles including the law of karma, justice and compassion. To write on spirituality is often a tedious job, for it is all inclusive and therefore, must involve apparent paradoxes. Moreover, one writes in time with particular references which are timeless, non-specific and beyond words. Yet, the writer has written in broad terms and integrates love and logic nicely.

Pray, may the sweet grace of the Lord saturate him evermore

Ever in His refuge,

– **Swami Prem Vivekananda**
Disciple of
Shri Chandra Swamiji Udasin
Sadhana Kendra Ashram
Domet, Dehradun

The Life of Shri Chandra Swami Udasin

Shri Chandra Swami Udasin was born on 5th of March, 1930, in the village Bhuman Shah, near Lahore (now Pakistan). Since childhood, he was blessed by the unreserved grace of his master Baba Bhuman Shahji, a great mystic and sage of the 18th century. Swamiji discontinued his post-graduate studies at the age of twenty-one and renounced all worldly ties. He passed eight years in seclusion and deep contemplation in Jammu & Kashmir. This was followed by another period of over nine years of solitude in sapta sarovar jhari, a forested island on the ganges near haridwar. It was here that he was blessed with the highest spiritual realization. In 1970, Swamiji shifted to sewak niwas, a small ashram in sapta sarovar. Twenty years later, he moved to the sadhana kendra ashram, located on the left bank of Yamuna, about fifty km from dehradun where he is staying presently. Shri Chandra Swamiji has large number of disciples and devotees in India and all over the world. Since 1984, he has been observing silence. In 1990, Life magazine (USA) had undertaken a worldwide survey entitled 'Men of God' and discovered nine sages from different countries. In its Dec 1991 edition, the magazine featured the nine sages. Beloved Chandra Swamiji was featured along with the revered Dalai Lama, his holiness Pope John Paul II and other saints.

Introduction

'Explore your potential' is a journey into Hinduism and an offshoot tradition of Buddhism namely Zen. The book is an effort to piece together the beautiful and profound wisdom of several sages which is scattered in the Vedas, several Upanishads and also esoteric works like Ananda Lahiri. This book will help the reader to get access to the wisdom in several scriptures in one piece. Several important concepts of Hinduism have been elaborated on. Several concepts of Shakti (Mother) worshipers have also been explained at length.

Zen has been discussed in this book because of its belief in non-dualistic consciousness which is same as the philosophy of Shakti worshippers. The book deals at length with the karma theory and explains in layman terms several profound secrets of the universe. Even some sutras which are normally only passed on in the oral tradition are documented in this book. Intuition and how it works have been elaborated on at length in this book and the secrets of developing intuitive perception have been revealed. Also I have posed Swamiji with nine eternal questions which have been debated for centuries and on which Swamiji has given brief pointed replies. To end the book on a creative note, there are four poems written by me as Salutation to 'The Divine Mother', 'The Guru', 'God' and 'The Seeker,' following which the fourty-one slokas of Ananda Lahiri (The wave of beauty and bliss) by Respected Sage Adi Shankaracharyaji have been elaborated on.

Contents

Summary of the Book — 11

Chapter – 1
Oral tradition in India — 24
The concept of the Mother — 24
The concept of Mother worship in the Hindu tradition — 25
The concept of sacrifice in Hinduism — 27
The nature of Gayatri — 27
The power of Mantras — 28
The meaning of Gayatri mantra — 28
The concept of warfare in Hinduism — 29
The goal of Mother worshipers — 30
The two main schools of Mother worshipers (Shakti Worship) — 30
The Ten Mahavidyas (branches of great knowledge) — 31
The Maha Mantra of Sri Vidya — 32
The Karma Theory — 33
Wisdom in Chapter I — 36

Chapter – 2
The eleven sutras of Hinduism — 40
Wisdom in chapter – II — 47

Chapter – 3
Intuition — 50
Intuition Versus Logic — 51
Intuition Over the Ages — 53
Exercises to enhance Intuitive perception — 54
Understanding the Trance state — 58
Wisdom in chapter – III — 59

Chapter – 4
1. Introduction to Zen — 62
2. Zen story — 62
   - It Will pass — 62
   - When tired — 62
   - Chasing two Rabbits — 63
   - Temper — 63
   - Nothing exists — 64
   - Zen dialogues — 64
   - The 360° Mind — 65
   - The Most Important Teaching — 65
   - Joshu Washes the Bowl — 66
   - Bodhidharma Pacifies the Mind — 66
   - The Mind Monarch — 66
   - Mystic Understanding — 68
   - Absolute Truth — 68
   - Truth and Words — 69
   - Life and Death — 69
3. Wisdom in Chapter – IV — 69

Chapter - 5
Life's Eternal Questions — 72

Chapter - 6
Mã — 79
The Seeker — 79
The Guru — 80
Bhagwãn — 81

Chapter - 7
Introduction to Ãnanda Lahari — 83
Forty-one Mantras of Ãnanda Lahari — 85
Wisdom of Chapter VII — 126

Glossary — **128**

Talk between Seeker Pappu and Sage Adveda

Talk between Seeker Pappu and Sage Adveda

Talk between Seeker Pappu and Sage Adveda

At this point Pappu the seeker bows before Sage Adveda and decides to read the book after all.

Man has evolved but his inner state is still primitive. We see Pappu above through Sage Adveda's Vision.

Zen Proverbs

The "way" is not difficult
For someone
Without preferences

Immersed in water,
You stretch out
Your hands for a drink.

Don't search for truth,
Simply stop having opinions.

Great understanding
Comes with great love.

Oral Tradition in India

In ancient times scriptures were passed on from the Guru to the disciple orally. The disciple had to remember all that the Guru said so that he could accurately pass on the same to his disciples. The impressionable sayings of the guru remained in the mind of the disciple whereas the mundane sayings although very important were never passed on. For example, if the Guru said, 'Death is just like the body changing old clothes'. All the disciples would remember it, but when the Guru spoke about love it was often considered mundane and a lot may never have been passed on. This book is an effort to piece together the beautiful and profound sayings of many gurus. Also, Sutras from Isha Upanishad and Mundaka Upanishad have been elaborated.

The Concept of the Mother

In simple words, worshipers of the Mother believe that the moment you believe in a concept, you are placing limitations on the mother.

Mother worshipers believe that the mother can feel the heart beat of all the species which exist in the universe created by her and yet it is inconceivable that you could actually get a glimpse of the mother. To get a glimpse of the mother, you need to move from the 'realm of calculation' to the 'realm of no calculation' and then proceed to the 'realm of anything is possible'. In simple terms, the Emperor can meet you any time but it is inconceivable, that you could walk into the Emperor's court. The 'zone of calculation' is a metaphor for new aspirants who have received the bija mantra, for such seekers the future lies in the realms of calculation. The 'zone of no calculation' is for seekers who have the Guru mantra. A future for such aspirants cannot be calculated. The 'zone of anything is possible,' is a metaphor for those praying to the mother.

Note : A bija is "a mantra consisting of one syllable with no ordinary meaning and always ending in the anusvara : m" The etiology of bijas is not known.(The origin of bijas is not known).

A bija mantra is usually given as the first initiation. The act of giving a bija mantra is like planting a seed in the soil and so it is called bija or seed mantra. The Guru mantra is usually the second initiation given (some precepts may have to be adhered to). Shakti worship is usually done by aspirants who have cleared the first two stages of initiation.

The Concept of Mother Worship in the Hindu Tradition

Mother worship in Hinduism is always done by the aspirant as a child, in front of the Mother Divine.

It is customary for the aspirant to pray to the Mother for something. Sages are of the belief that anyone praying to the mother apparently for nothing could be unconsciously lying because we are dependant on the Mother for everything. However, there could be cases of highly evolved sages who may want nothing for themselves.

There are three types of Mother worship done by sages as differentiated by the short-term motive, although long-term motive is always meant to experience the non-dualistic consciousness.

(a) **Sages who pray for knowledge**
This school of thought makes uses of the Gayatri mantra. The Gayatri mantra is the Mother of the Vedas. Sages of this order believe there is nothing higher than knowledge and that it should be the goal of the aspirant.

(b) Sages who pray for something specific

Many sages want something specific from the Mother and so use specific mantras. An example of this is Shankaracharya's 'Soundarya Lahiri' where specific mantras are given for specific relief or benefit.

(c) Sages who pray for Mother's love

This is a highly secretive sect and records are usually preserved only in oral tradition.

This sect rejects knowledge as something worth praying for. They believe that knowledge can be dual, i.e., can cause pleasure as well as give pain, e.g., knowledge of past lives can be a source of pleasure as well as pain.

In general, Hindu Sages reject the concept of eternal heaven and eternal hell and they believe that everything is bound by time and space. This is the underlying basis for the theory of karma which the sages propagated and believed in. The sages of mother worship also do not believe in eternal hell and heaven but they do believe in God who can give things which are eternal. For example - God may grant a seeker with a very good voice eternally but it is possible that he may not receive recognition for that voice in his lifetime and therefore the good voice may not be a source of joy in his life time. These sages believe that gifts are unimportant; only love is important. On this basis, the sages of this tradition reject even creativity as being something worth praying for.

Also, the sages of this tradition believe that everything in this universe is dual and only Mothers love is one sided. An often cited sutra by the sages of this tradition is 'The universe bows before love, mankind is ultimately in search of love - for love is evolution'.

I am proud to say that I have met two sages who emanate only love. They are Chandra Swamiji Udasin and Chote Swami (Swami Prem Vivekanand). All the views expressed herein are views of the sages of this order who believe in praying for Mother's love.

The Concept of Sacrifice in Hinduism

Sacrifice forms a very important part of the Hindu mythology. In Hindu mythology when samudra manthan (churning of the ocean) was done, the practice was to give first and then receive. Many demi-gods chose to sacrifice animals and even their loved ones to please God. Mother Gayatri chose differently, she chose not to sacrifice but to protect, and for that different thought process she is remembered as the Mother of Vedas. The Goddesses of Intelligence chose to sacrifice their weak points in return for love from God. The principle of giving first unconditionally and then receiving is the corner stone of the Hindu mythology. When you give, you taste the Amrit (the true nectar). The mantra of Mother Gayatri is

> *Om Bhur Bhuvah Swah*
> *Tat savitur vareniyam*
> *Bhargo devasya dhimahi*
> *Dhiyo Yona Prachodayat*

The mantra acts as a catalyst for transformation. The mantra works on the subtle impressions in our unconscious mind and helps us gain correct perception. This is a mantra for the masses because the divine force behind the mantra does not discriminate or judge the practitioner as worthy or unworthy of practising the mantra. This is so because the Mother does not discriminate between her children or judge them. This mantra can be practised without adhering to any precepts. When the time is ripe the mantra transforms and guides the aspirant forward.

The Nature of Gayatri

The word Gayatri is used in Hindu scriptures in three different senses. Firstly, for the well-known mantra, secondly, for the meter in which the mantra is cast and thirdly, for the Goddess who wields the power of the mantra. According to the Hindu philosophy, in unmanifest reality, only Brahman exists but when manifestation takes place Brahman is split between Shiva and Shakti, and Shakti is further split into the various functions it performs in the universe. This gives rise to deities (gods and goddesses). Mother Gayatri liberates souls from the bondage of maya. (Shiva stands for consciousness and Shakti for power).

The Power of Mantras

Mantras have the power to remove ignorance, reveal the truth and help realize moksha. The meaningfulness of mantras is not merely intellectual.

As Vyasa puts it:-

The yogi who has come to know well the relation between word and meaning must constantly repeat it and habituate the mind to the manifestation therein of its meaning. The constant repetition is to be of the Pranava and the habitual mental manifestation is to be that of what it signifies (Ishwara). The mind of the yogi who constantly repeats the Pranava and habituates the mind to the constant manifestation of the idea it carries, becomes one pointed.

The Meaning of Gayatri Mantra

The literal translation is "may be obtained that desirable radiance of God Savitar who is to impel our visions." However, later, 'dhi' (to think) has been reinterpreted as 'dhya' (which means to meditate) and now the popular translation is 'May we meditate on the lovely splendour of God Savitar so he may inspire our mind". This is because of the high importance attached to Dhyana by the later seers and the firm belief that the identification with the object of concentration resulted in 'obtaining' that object by way of identification. In any case, it became the 'Shema' of brahmanical religion and instruction and its utterance is central to the upanayana ceremony of initiation for the 'twice born'.

The Concept of Warfare in Hinduism

From the interpretation of many Hindu mythological stories and the Bhagvad Gita we can conclude, that the Hindus believe that war is allowed on the following grounds:

(a) In the name of God - where there is no personal gain whatsoever in form of property or ego.
(b) To protect your own self respect - it may be necessary to fight a battle if you are attacked.
(c) Injustice - if you perceive great injustice it may be necessary to intervene and protect people.

Many Hindu mythological stories reveal that in the above three cases if you do not fight then you may be judged by God as a crawly insect. However, the above three grounds should not be used as a reason to go to war because change in time, place and circumstances may change everything.

The sages reiterate:
(a) God needs no protection so there is no need to go to war on these grounds.
(b) It is God's universe and you need not go to war every time you perceive a threat to your self respect.
(c) There can be no injustice in the universe if you truly believe in God.

The sages reiterate that truth is then only perception and a God loving person can never be touched. But these are the words of sages who have tasted the Divine first hand, experienced His omnipotence and omniscience. For others, the pairs of opposites like good and bad exist.

The Goal of Mother Worshipers

The goals of the mother worshipers are:-
(a) Surrender to God
(b) Trust in God
(c) Faith in God
(d) Love for God

The essence is that all life is an effort to build on your surrender, trust, faith and love for God. When sadhana is done, incorporating these four principles, the sadhak experiences non-dual consciousness.

Mother worshipers believe that surrender, trust, faith and love for God is not mere lip service but must reflect in your karma. They believe that surrender to God is not true surrender until it is tested. Surrender, trust, faith and love for God are the end-points man wants to reach. Once you understand the goal, the journey is enjoyable.

The Two Main Schools of Mother Worshipers (Shakti Worship)

There are two main schools of Shakti worship namely, Samaya and Kaula. To experience oneness with the Mother or non-dualistic consciousness is the goal of both the schools of Shakti worshipers. What is different is the sadhana undertaken in order to experience this oneness.

The Kaula School believes in external rituals. They use liquor, meat, fish, mudras and physical union in their rituals. Also they use external physical yantras whereas the Samaya school views the body as a Yantra. They have purely yogic practices and do not believe in external rituals.

Some commentators such as Lakshmidhara have regarded the Kaula school as 'Avaidika' because the Kaulas use liquor, meat, fish, mudras and physical union in their rituals. However, the masters say it is not right to condemn either of the schools of worship. Both the schools will ultimately lead us to the one ultimate reality. To be able to analyze or understand the Kaula school of worship we need to have an unbiased mind which is not conditioned by what we believe to be right or wrong.

The masters say perception about right and wrong changes with time, place and circumstances.

However, worship done with strict adherence to precepts as done by the Samaya school is always recommended by the masters.

The Ten Mahavidyas
(Branches of Great Knowledge)

There are ten Mahavidyas in Shakti worship. The goal of Shakti worship is to realize the oneness with the mother. Each Vidya is distinct and helps the aspirant to realize a particular aspect of Mother, 'the one ultimate reality'.

The Mahavidyas are:
- (1) Kali — (aspect is might)
- (2) Tara — (aspect is sound force)
- (3) Bhuvnesvari — (aspect is vast vision)
- (4) Bhairavi — (aspect is charm)
- (5) Chinnamasta — (aspect is striking force)
- (6) Dhumavati — (aspect is silent inertness)
- (7) Bagalamukhi — (aspect is power)
- (8) Matangi — (aspect is expressive play)
- (9) Kamala — (aspect is harmony)
- (10) Sodasi — (aspect is beauty and bliss)

The Maha Mantra of Sri Vidya

Maha Tripura Sundari is the ultimate, primordial shakti, the light of manifestation. She, the pile of letters of the alphabet, gave birth to the three worlds. At dissolution, She is the abode of all tatvas, still remaining herself.

- Vamakeshvaratantra

Hindus believe that the following mantra, if chanted with love, can lead to fulfillment of all desires including realization of oneness with the Mother.

Ka ei La Hrim	(Vagbhava)
Ha sa ka ha la hrim	(Kamaraja)
Saka La Hrim	(Rudra Shakti)
Shreem	(Shambu Nath)

Inner meaning

The secret is that there is no one else, only the Mother exists. The Vidya shows oneness of Shiva, Guru, Devi and disciple, as it is Shiva in sound form (Shakti) who preserves the line.

Lalita means she who plays. All creation, manifestation and dissolution are considered to be a play of the Devi or the Goddess. Mahatripura Sundari is her name, as transcendent beauty of the three lokas (waking, dreaming and deep sleep).

There are many variations of the Sri Vidya mantra. The mantra is the variation that Laksmidhara gives in his commentary and has fifteen syllables. Laxmidhara added the syllable 'Shreem' and called it Sri Vidya. There is another school of thought which believes that the 16th syllable is the soundless sound. These gurus purposely make a mockery of all duality by referring to the soundless sound. To realize the soundless sound which lies beyond all duality is the goal of the Sri Vidya Mantra. When you go beyond sound, you realize the truth in silence. When you go beyond sound and silence, you are in the realm of pure love and that is the 16th syllable of Sri Vidya, i.e., the fifteen syllables uttered with love.

This school of thought firmly believes that the 16th syllable of the Sri Vidya mantra lies beyond the realm of sound and silence. Orthodox practitioners of the Sri Vidya believe that your soul can be given but the 16th syllable of the mantra can never be given except to a very exceptional disciple. However, many gurus believe that it does not matter if you give the sixteenth syllable or not because the divine forces behind the mantra weed out the unworthy.

The Karma Theory

What is karma and how does it work?
The karma theory is, explained in simplistic terms, 'As you sow so shall you reap'.

Karma is neither fatalism nor a doctrine of predetermination. The past influences the present but does not dominate it, for karma is past as well as present. The past and present influence the future. The past is the background against which life goes on from moment to moment. The future is yet to be.

The Buddha defined kamma or karma as – "mental volition, O Bhikkhus is what I call action" (karma).

Having volition on acts by the body, speech and thought.

(Anguttara Nikaya III 415)

Lord Buddha believed that everything was not a result of past karma and that the laws of the universe ran parallel with the karma theory.

Let us explain the karma theory in simple terms-
Suppose you take a taxi from one destination to another. You know you have to pay as per the meter. Suppose the fare is Rs.100/- now as soon as you pay Rs.100/- there is no further liability on you or alternatively someone else with Rs100/- could gift it to you to discharge the liability. Then also your liability stands discharged. The karma theory presupposes a few things. They are:-

(a) The consequences of every action are well defined and fixed in advance.
(b) The consequences of every action are known consciously or unconsciously to all and are equal to all.
(c) The consequences of every action may vary from place to place or time to time but they would in principle be equal to all, e.g., if you eat in a five star hotel the charges would be different than what you would pay for food in a dhaba, but the charges of both the places are known in advance to all and are same for all visitors there.

Some seers have gone ahead and explained the karma theory in greater detail. They believe that karma does not have to be set off from person to person. They believe that karmas are converted into 'love credits' and your balance of 'love credits' determines what you get in the universe. They believe money, fame, power, knowledge, charisma etc. are just openings for love to enter your life. The often repeated sutra of this tradition is 'The Universe is in search of love - for love is evolution'. If you desire anything in the universe your 'love credit' balance is checked and if you have the balance you might get it. In simplistic terms, they believe that the universe is like a vacation spot and 'credits' are being added and deducted all the time.

Some important assumptions by the seers of this tradition are:-
  (a) **Love is measurable -** They explain this by saying that put your own child and someone else's child in front and you know whom you love more. Even gurus know which disciple loves them more. The sages of this tradition therefore believe that God is the only Guru because only he can be equal to all or know who is more deserving.
  (b) Love exists within time and space and is also transient.
  (c) Your karma is measured on exact parameters which are same for all. For example, in a class room, attendance, internal projects and external exams are often parameters. Similarly everybody's karmas are judged on exactly same parameters. However, how you are judged may depend on which class you are in. For example, 5th std. papers would be different from 10th std. papers. The boards may vary, e.g., SSC papers are at different level from ICSE papers. The moot point is allowance is made for the level of consciousness of the person whose karmas are being judged and accordingly love credits are added or subtracted.

To sum up, karma is important and the person is himself writing his own destiny.

At this point many thinkers would ask if only karma is important - why pray to God? Where does God fit in?

The simple answer given by the sages is, that the moment you assume karma is important and the Universe is equal to all you presuppose there does exist a higher force who ensures that things are equal to all. To believe in the karma theory, your first assumption has to be that God exists.

The second question which arises is that if God is equal to all then he is a God bound by rules. For example, if you do a good deed and the prize for the deed is one sweet, then everyone who does that deed gets one piece of sweet. What kind of a God is He who has no discretion? Why pray to God who has no discretion to help?

The belief of the sages on this point is, 'God would overturn the Universe for love'. Therefore, if you really love God there is nothing he would not do for you. However, the caveat is that if anyone's love went beyond that point He would do the same for them, in that overall sense God would be equal to all.

Wisdom in Chapter I

1. There are infinite ways to pray to the Mother. All ways are acceptable to the Mother.
2. The universe bows before love, mankind is ultimately in search of love, for love is evolution.
3. The Gayatri mantra is an ideal tool for concentration and can be practised without adhering to any precept.
4. 'Giving unconditionally' is the corner stone of Hindu mythology.
5. The weak sacrifice, the strong are the protectors.
6. Perception about right and wrong depends on time, place and circumstances.

7. Your philosophy must reflect in your actions.
8. The Maha mantra of Sri Vidya is revealed in this chapter. It is usually not advisable to practise this mantra without the proper guidance of a Guru. This is usually practised at the third stage by people who have cleared the first two stages of initiation, i.e., the Bija mantra and Guru mantra.
9. Do good and good things will happen to you.
10. Karma is not set off from person to person. It is not a barter system but more like a monetary system.
11. God would overturn the universe for love.

Quotes of Dalai Lama

Be kind whenever possible.
It is always possible.

In the practice of tolerance,
One's enemy is the best teacher.

The purpose of our lives is to be happy
We can live without religion and meditation,
but we cannot survive without human affection.

We can never obtain peace in the outer world until
we make peace with ourselves.

The Eleven Sutras of Hinduism

Sutra -1

The Universe spins on love and surrender to God
(Oral Tradition)

Respected sage Shankaracharyaji described Maya as the illusionary power of the Brahman. The seers of the third order (who believe in praying to the mother for love only) do not doubt this; however they also say Maya is love. Love is the substance with which this illusion is spun. Whether you go deep in the universe or deep within you cannot go beyond love. When love is strong and develops into faith, truth will unfold. They believe that at the first stage the mother will offer love only through toys like siddhis (extraordinary powers) and slowly the truth will unfold because a relationship cannot be strong unless there is truth in it. Therefore truth cements the relationship further.

A similar view is expressed in the Isha Upanishad.

'The face of truth is covered with a golden veil. Truth unfolds if love is genuine; God knows the past, present, future and is wise, therefore the sages advocate surrender to God. Sometimes you may want something badly but may never get it - This is so because God knows what is best for you. In time you may get something better. Surrender implies trust and faith in God.

Sutra – 2

(Oral tradition)
All paths merge into one, the path of love.

The sages believe that different religions, different paths within each religion are all different ways of expressing love for God. It does not matter which method you use to express love for God as long as you express it.

Sutra - 3
Verse - 12 - Mundaka Upanishad

After examining the objects of the world that one has gained through one's karma, the aspirant reaches a state of dispassion and non-attachment and realizes that the highest cannot be attained through mere actions. In order to know that, the aspirant should present himself, with all humility, to a guru who is learned and established in Brahman consciousness.

This appears contradictory if you believe that only God can be the guru because only God can be equal to all and only God can know who has merit and who has not. In truth it is not contradictory. The blessing of the sages are over flowing and often the sages give what God would not and in the scheme of the Universe, it cannot be questioned because it was theirs to give. Fortunate are those who have the blessings of the sages because the love of the sages is always eternal. They find ways to give even when you do not have the capacity to receive. I bow down before all the sages not because they have reached the truth but because inspite of having seen the truth they emanate only love and compassion for fellow beings.

Sutra - 4
Isha Upanishad - Second pada verse 6

But he who sees all beings in the self and the self in all beings ceases to have hatred for anyone.

The essence of this sutra is that one who has realized this has no hatred for anyone and emanates only love and compassion.

Sutra - 5

Isha Upanishad - Third pada verses 9 to 11

9. Those devoted to illusion enter blind darkness; into greater darkness enter those who are solely attached to knowledge.
10. One thing is obtained from knowledge, another from illusion. Thus we have heard from the wise who have taught us.
11. Knowledge and illusion, he who knows both, overcomes death through illusion, and through knowledge enjoys immortality.

To understand illusion it is important to understand why illusion exists. It is important to know that the rules of the universe are so because of love.

Examples are as follows:

Everyone in this universe dies but we have short memories and so very soon we forget the loved ones we lost and carry on with our lives. Thus, our short memories are so because the rules of the Universe are laced with love.

We all have to die but our minds are configured in such a way that we never think of death, otherwise life would be unbearable.

We don't know the date of our death. This is a blessing because life would otherwise be unbearable.

These are the examples of how the rules of the Universe are laced with mother's love.

Illusion exists because of love, and knowledge is also received because of love. One who has seen both darkness and light, knows why things are how they are; he overcomes the fear of death and gains immortality.

Sutra – 6

(Oral tradition)
Who am I?

Many schools of Indian thought use "Who am I?" as a contemplative tool to realize their own essential nature and also realize the possibility of continuous evolution and transformation.

Mankind is created with the 'I', and every action of man is centered on protecting the 'I' and everything connected with 'I'. If this was not the primary tendency of mankind, our civilization would have ceased to exist long back. Either you interfere with the course of mankind every now and then or create people in such a way that they protect themselves. Similarly, sex is a primary tendency of mankind so that civilization exists on a continuous basis.

My Gurudev's words are

'I am whatever he would want me to be, a truth greater than that I cannot see'.

My Gurudev believes there is no point in contemplation on "Who am I?", if no effort is made to transform yourself and become what you would be proud to be.

You could have all the accomplishments known to man, but without God's grace and the Guru's blessing, your life would be a miserable existence indeed.

Sutra - 7

Another important sutra of oral tradition.

Love will find love,

Manipulation will meet manipulation.

The sages repeat this sutra many times over. Planning, plotting, clever executing, sweet talking, impressive dressing and using of psychology to impress others are essentials in the material world but in the spiritual world they are your undoing because your motives are known. You always stand nude before God. A person who truly loves God will find God. A manipulator will be manipulated. Love is a funny commodity. The sages say. The more you give away, the more you have.

Sutra - 8
Ananda - Lahari verse I

Shiva-shaktiya-yukto Yadhi Bhavathi Shakthaha Prabhavithum
Na Chel-evam Devo Na Khalu Kushalaha Spandhithum-api
Atha-s-tuaam-aaradhyaam Hari-hara-virincha-aadibhir-api
Prananthum Sthothum Vaa Kadham-akrutha-punyha   Prabhavathi

Sage Shankaracharyji in verse 1 of Ananda Lahari says that only a few meritorious people have the right to pray to mother, who, even the gods adore and worship.

Background

The seers believed that nothing in the universe is impossible. For this to be true they believed that if you believe something to be true, its reverse must also be true. The sages believed that God is equally accessible to all but for this to be true, God is accessible to only a few should also be true.

If nothing is impossible for God, and therefore, for something to be true its reverse must also be true, then the question to be asked is, 'what about death?" Because everyone dies and the reverse that a few people don't die is not true.

The sages say that in the truest sense there is no death, and being nine months in a mother's womb, death is just a set of entry and exit rules for mankind, and the rules have to be respected. They also add that just because nothing is impossible for God, He does not have to prove it in every case.

This sutra is described in greater detail later on in the book where each of the forty-one verses of the Ananda Lahari has been commented on.

※※

Sutra - 9
Oral Tradition

'I come from nowhere, to nowhere will I go; if I define nowhere you will know what I know.'

Here Gurudev tries to break the logical thinking patterns of the mind. Logic is an invalid tool in the search of truth as logic can be applied only when all the infinite parameters are known. When some things are known and some unknown, logic would only help us to arrive at faulty results. Correct perception is the valid tool in the search for truth. If I owe you zero rupees you gain nothing and yet it is zero which has propelled mathematics to the next level.

A similar sutra is found in the Brihad Aranyaka Upanishad (1.2.1), "In the beginning there was nothing". The thought process is that everything comes out of nothing and goes back into nothing and that in truth only Brahman exists. Brahman is the one without a second.

※※

Sutra - 10
The Sutra of Tantric Tradition

'Pig's droppings are as good as name, fame and honour; being hailed as a Guru is mere noise; ego is another from of drunkenness. Only after renouncing these three, one truly remembers the name of God'.

The tantrics believe in this sutra but they believe that the reverse is also true.

The logic is....

Every thing that man has today is a result of work done by someone else, e.g., he lives in a house built by someone, eats food grown by some one else. Man would have remained a primitive animal had a system of systemized passing on of knowledge not been developed. This is because man shares everything he has with others. Had man been built with no desire for name, fame and honour, man would not have readily shared his knowledge with others as he would have desired nothing. Mankind has an ego and this results in a win / win situation. The person sharing benefits and the person with whom it is shared also benefits.

Sharing is at the core of creation. Mankind is like a tower being built - people build on work done by others and there is no limit to how high the tower can go.

Sutra - 11
Isha Upanishad
Fourth pada
18th Sutra

Agni, lead me by the good path to the fruits of my actions. Deva, you know all deeds. Remove me from the fault of deceit. I offer myriad words of devotion to you.

This is an expression of the last desire of the seeker on his death bed. This is a prayer offered right at the end and therefore, has been chosen as the last sutra for the Upanishad.

The seeker prays to God that he develops good qualities, the subtle impression of which will be carried forward from life to life and not pay attention to that which is temporary and which will be left behind in this world.

Wisdom in Chapter – II

1. The universe spins on love and surrender to God.
2. All paths merge into one the path of love.
3. The highest cannot be known by karmas (actions) alone and when one realizes this he begins his spiritual journey.
4. One who has realized non-duality can emanate only love.
5. The rules of the universe are laced with love.
6. Contemplation is a valid tool on the spiritual path but is of less use if your karmas (actions) are not good. If your karma is good, contemplation is a gift from the Guru within.
7. You can manipulate the world but not God.
8. Nothing is impossible in this universe. You have heard it many times but only the unconditioned mind truly believes it.
9. God is equal and yet unequal. Everyone dies but very few truly live.
10. Logic is a valid tool only if all the infinite factors are known. The only truly valid tool is intuition.
11. Ego is good, desires are good. It all depends on your perception. Everything has its uses.
12. Sharing is at the core of creation.
13. You are a visitor in this Universe what you accumulate will be left behind.

Quotes of Buddha

A jug fills drop by drop.

All wrong - doing arises because of mind.

If mind is transformed, can wrong doing remain?

Hatred does not cease by hatred, but only by love, this is the eternal rule.

He is able who thinks he is able.

I do not believe in a fate that falls on men however they act, but I do believe in a fate that falls on them unless they act.

I never see what has been done, I only see what remains to be done.

The way is not in the sky. The way is in the heart.

Intuition

What is intuition?

Intuition is immediate apprehension of the mind, without any logical reasoning. The word 'intuition' comes from the Latin word 'intueri' which is often roughly translated to as meaning 'to look inside' or 'to contemplate'.

How does it work?

Our mind has many features and facets that we are not ordinarily aware about. As we purify our mind, we begin the process of self discovery. Just like you may own a cell phone which has many features but you may use it only for talking to people as you are not aware of how to use the other features.

We normally use our mind only for basic tasks since we are not aware or taught a systematized manner of increasing the range or the reach of the human mind.

Everything mankind has achieved is because it has developed a systematized method of passing on knowledge. Had it not been for education, man still would have been a primitive animal. However, due to the nature and needs of man, education is focused around earning a livelihood. Man has physical, emotional and a psychological need due to which 'inner research' has largely been ignored as it is not profitable in the world we live in. Also transferring the knowledge received is difficult as our mental conditioning and religious beliefs can prove to be a hindrance.

Intuition is in layman terms 'knowing the truth when logic and facts may point in another direction'.

How does our mind function?

All human experience is associated with some form of editing of the full account of reality. Our senses prune the amount of information received. Our mind gathers information, edits it and then seeks to extract patterns from this information.

It is estimated that a trillion bits of information enter our senses every second but only a fraction of it enters our conscious mind. The balance remains in our unconscious mind. When the mind is calm and receptive, the information comes forward from our unconscious mind to conscious mind.

Profitable uses of intuition
- To predict prices of gold or other commodities.
- To predict movements of stock market.
- To take decisions regarding property.
- To take other important decisions.

Who is intuitive?

Everybody is intuitive at some time or the other in his or her life but very few people consciously use intuition. There are some people who have a well-developed sense of intuition; this is normally due to work done in previous lifetime or work done consciously to become more intuitive.

Intuition Versus Logic

Intuition is a phenomenon that cannot be explained scientifically. It lies beyond the realm of the intellect. When the mind is still, the truth is known in silence. Logic has limited application. For logic to help us to arrive at a solution, all the factors affecting the decision must be known. In a universe like ours, there are infinite factors both known and unknown, hence logic may not always be a valid tool to arrive at the correct answer. Intuition is that which lies beyond the realm of the intellect. The intellect is severely limited because it tries to reach a solution based on facts that are known when in reality there are several factors which are unknown. To cope with change, we must rely on intuition rather than logic which lies beyond the realm of the intellect. When you are unconscious, you function by instinct, e.g., survival is an instinct. When you are conscious, you use the intellect and in a state of super consciousness, you use intuition. The Shiva Sutras say, 'Gyanam Bandhanam' which means knowledge is bondage. Knowledge helps us to function in the world with our eyes closed. It is like driving a car while looking at the back seat. The idea is to not be a slave to accumulated knowledge but to be 'open' to receiving what the universe has to offer. When you do not have accumulated knowledge, you have a childlike innocence, your mind is not conditioned nor do you have any prejudices. Intuition is one of the most mysterious and beautiful things which the universe has to offer – you know, but you don't know how or why. Somehow the individual consciousness has come into contact with the universal consciousness and the unexplainable has happened in silence. The mind has transcended all the barriers and made contact with the universal consciousness, and in that state the truth is known.

Everybody makes this contact some time or the other unconsciously, but the Sages consciously make contact and this experience is called Samadhi (state of super consciousness).

Normal ways to develop intuition:
(A) The shortcut (japa or God remembrance)

Japa or chanting God's name, or God remembrance in any form is regarded as a shortcut to developing siddhis like intuition. Through the practice of japa, the mind and senses are purified, the obstacles are removed and one can see reality as it is.

(B) The mind control route

Empty your thoughts and try to increase the gap between two successive thoughts. This must be done daily over a long period of time.

The aspirant must also develop love, compassion and be engrossed in virtuous acts if this route is to be adopted, whereas if you are practicing japa, purification of mind is automatic.

(C) The flame gazing, water gazing or shadow gazing route

The Delphic and the Branchidic oracles used flame gazing and water gazing to enter trance states. Several tantrics use shadow gazing to enter similar states. It is said Nostradamus used contemplation, meditation and incubation (i.e., ritually 'sleeping on it') to enter the trance state, however, there is a popular legend that he also used the ancient methods of fire and water gazing.

(D) The concentration on breath route

This method has been used by many adepts (including the Buddha) over a period of time with several variations. This is the most natural method of concentration. Each aspirant can develop his own method of breath concentration.

Intuition Over the Ages

In 2000 BC, Egyptian oracles practised dream incubation techniques for stroking intuition. They slept in special temples in the hope of inducing divinely inspired dreams.

In China, a few hundred years later tortoise shells were tossed into fire and the resulting cracks in the shells were read as omens about future events.

In 650 BC, Delphic oracles at the Temple of Apollo in Greece used to foretell the future through God Apollo. Priestess Pythia only gave predictions on the seventh of every month as seven was the number associated with God Apollo. Pythia inhaled vapours rising up through the cracks in the temple's floor to induce an altered state of consciousness. Then in this trance state, she responded to queries regarding the future. In order to test her and all the other oracles of that time, King Croesus of Lydia devised a test. He chopped a lamb and a tortoise and boiled them together in a cauldron of brass and covered it with a lid of brass. Pythia was the only oracle who was accurate. In fact her accuracy was so striking that Croesus consulted her about what would happen if he invaded Persia. She replied in a traditional hexameter verse 'that if you cross the river, it would destroy a great empire' Croesus assumed he would win and invaded Persia. He lost the war and a great empire was destroyed, only it was his own.

When dealing with oracles it is important to frame the question properly and check your assumptions.

Michel de Nostredame (1503-1566) usually latinized to Nostradamus, was a French apothecary physician and reputed seer who published a collection of prophesies that have since become famous worldwide. The sole description of the process he used to enter trance states is contained in letter forty-one of his collected Latin correspondence. It is doubtful that he used any method other than contemplation, meditation and incubation. However, there is a popular legend that he also used the method of flame gazing and water gazing. In his dedication to King Henry II, Nostradamus describes his method as, "emptying my soul, mind and heart of all care, worry and unease through mental calm and tranquility".

Exercises to Enhance Intuitive Perception

Exercise 1
Japa method
Aim: To purify the mind
Requirements:
- Sit in a comfortable chair.

- Chant the mantra using any of the techniques given below.
- Concentrate for at least ten minutes.

Techniques;
- A. Visualization: Visualize the words of the mantra in your mind.
- B. Hearing the mantra: Listen to the sound of the mantra through your inner ear.
- C. Coordinating the mantra with your natural breathing

Exercise 2
Centering your consciousness
Aim: Helps in living in the present moment and building dispassion
Requirements:
- Sit in a comfortable chair

Techniques:
1. Take a few moments to contemplate the moment.
2. Close your eyes and listen to the sounds and hear them as pure sounds only.
3. Become aware of your body sensations and the temperature of the room.
4. Become aware of your breath.
5. Now as your breath becomes even, start witnessing your thoughts.
6. Do not judge the thoughts, accept everything, reject nothing.
7. Mind will wander away, bring it back to witness consciousness.

Exercise 3
Developing compassion
Aim: – To develop empathy and love

- Self healing

Requirements:
- Sit in a comfortable chair.

Technique:
1. Think of someone or something you hate.
2. Visualize that person or thing in your mind.
3. Let the feeling of love arise.
4. Forgive, and help your mind come to a more neutral stance, conquering negative emotions.

Exercise 4
Live in awareness
Aim: To make choices consciously
Requirements:
- Sit in a comfortable chair

Technique:
1. See every object in the room.
2. Be aware of the sounds in the room.
3. Gain a sense of shape, colour and presence of things.
4. Concentrate for at least five minutes on things in the room.
5. You can end by offering a prayer and be grateful for life.

Exercise 5
Mind
Aim: To develop an open mind
Requirements:
1. Sit in a comfortable chair with the back straight
2. Do gentle stretching exercises

Technique:
1. Be aware of your breath.

2. Once the breath is even, start trying to stop your thoughts and try to increase the gap between two thoughts.
3. Once the conscious mind is relaxed, then the impressions from the unconscious mind will come forward.

This method is mentioned in the yoga sutras by Patanjali and is generally used to gain knowledge about past lives.

Exercise 6
Wall gazing
Aim: To have greater mind control
Requirements:
− Sit in a comfortable chair facing the wall

Technique:
1. Put a small dot (or use a bindi) against the wall at your eye level.
2. The distance between you and the wall must be half your height.
3. Concentrate on the dot on the wall.
4. Try to increase your capacity to five minutes.

This method was used by Bodhi Dharma to enter trance states.

Exercise 7

Mind control through visualization

This technique is used by martial artist to deny pain as they shift the focus of their mind.
Aim: To focus the mind consciously
Requirements:
− Sit in a comfortable chair or lie down.

Technique:
1. Close your eyes and be aware of your breath.
2. Slowly draw attention of the mind to each body part, one at a time.

3. Now shift the attention of the mind to a beautiful beach and visualize the scenery.
4. Now shift the attention of the mind to any place you have been in the past and found beautiful.
5. Open your eyes.

Exercise 8
The Koan/contemplation method
Aim: To break logical pattern of the mind
Requirements:
Sit in a comfortable chair with eyes closed
Technique:
1. Select any koan as a contemplation tool or use 'who am I?'
2. Concentrate on the koan.
3. Record your insights.
4. When the mind becomes one pointed, the koan's essence is revealed.

Understanding the Trance State

Without realising it most of us already know what a trance is like. Natural trance occurs during moments of intense concentration or creativity, e.g., when you are engrossed in some work you may not realize how much time has passed.

Stephen T. Gilligan says 'the state of trance is biologically essential for all human beings'. Not only is trance experienced in many situations, e.g., daydreaming, dancing, watching a movie, etc., – but it is also induced in many different ways. Trance can be induced through rhythmic and repetitive movement; through chanting and prayer; through massage; through drugs, etc. All these methods tend to decrease the cacophony of conscious awareness with its discontinuous patterns of stimulation.

Tips to use the eight exercises
- (a) Let the mind put no resistance in trying out the exercises. The mind will come up with excuses like, this will not work for me or I know some of these practices, so what's new? The first step is therefore, to overcome the resistance of the mind.
- (b) You must flow with the experience. To be able to flow with the experience, one must be totally relaxed and enjoy the experience. In order to be totally relaxed, the following would help:
  - (i) Do the exercises at a time when there are fewer disturbances in the surroundings.
  - (ii) Your clothing must be comfortable.
  - (iii) The place must be quiet so that you are not disturbed.

Wisdom in Chapter – III

1. Everyone is intuitive, some unconsciously, some consciously.
2. Intuition has profitable uses, and so an aspirant on the spiritual path can live comfortably in this word. So it is a myth that inner research is not profitable.
3. It may be difficult to transfer the knowledge received as a result of inner research to others, but the methods used can be passed on.
4. Our mind has many features and facets we are not ordinarily aware about. As we purify our mind, we begin the process of self discovery.
5. Accumulated knowledge can be bondage as our mind is conditioned and limited.

Quotes

To disbelieve is easy, to scoff is simple,
To have faith is harder.

- Louis L'almour

I am the wisest man alive, for I know one thing, and that is that I know nothing.

- Socrates

Hope is the dream of a waking man.

- Aristotle

At the touch of Love everyone becomes a poet.

- Plato

Death is not the worst that can happen to men.

- Plato

1. Introduction to Zen

Our senses provide us with an edited version of reality, e.g., we hear sounds at certain frequencies only, we can see only if a certain degree of light is present, etc.

In Zen, enlightenment implies oneness with the Universe and liberation from dualism which our mind perceives to be the truth. Zen masters make an effort to uproot the logical thinking process of their disciples, and once the barriers are removed, the disciples sees the universe as it is. Zen masters emphasize that the truth cannot be taught through words and must be understood intuitively as words have their limitations in conveying the true meaning.

2. Zen Story

It Will Pass

A student went to his meditation teacher and said, "My meditation is horrible! I feel so distracted."

The teacher said - "It will pass."

A month later, the student came back to his teacher and said, "My meditation is wonderful! I feel so aware."

The teacher said - "It will pass."

When Tired

A student once asked his teacher

"Master, what is enlightenment?"

The master replied,

"When hungry, eat, when tired, sleep".

Chasing Two Rabbits

A martial arts student approached his teacher with a question.

"In order to improve my knowledge of martial arts in addition to learning from you, I'd like to study with another teacher. What do you think of the idea?"

The master replied "The hunter who chases two rabbits catches neither one".

Temper

A Zen student came to Bankei and complained: 'Master, I have an ungovernable temper. How can I cure it?'

'You have something very strange', replied Bankei, 'Let me see what you have'.

'Just now I cannot show it to you', replied the other.

'When can you show it to me?' asked Bankei.

'It arises unexpectedly', replied the student.

'Then', concluded Bankei, 'it must not be your own true nature. If it were, you could show it to me at any time. When you were born you did not have it, and your parents did not give it to you. Think that over'.

Nothing Exists

Yamaoka Tesshu, as a young student of Zen, visited one master after another. He called upon Dokuon of Shokoku.

Desiring to show his attainment, he said: 'The mind, Buddha, and sentient beings, after all, do not exist. The true nature of phenomena is emptiness. There is no realization, no delusion, no sage, and no mediocrity. There is no giving and nothing to be received.'

Dokuon, who was smoking quietly, said nothing. Suddenly he whacked Yamaoka with his bamboo pipe. This made the youth quite angry.

'If nothing exists', inquired Dokuon, 'where did this anger come from?'

Zen Dialogues

Zen teachers train their young pupils to express themselves. Two Zen temples had each a child protégé. One child, going to obtain vegetables each morning, would meet the other on the way.

'Where are you going?', asked one.

'I am going wherever my feet go', the other responded.

This reply puzzled the first child who went to his teacher for help. 'Tomorrow morning', the teacher told him, 'when you meet that little fellow, ask him the same question. He will give you the same answer, and then you ask him: "Suppose you have no feet, then where are you going?" That will fix him'.

The children met again the following morning.

'Where are you going?' asked the first child.

'I am going wherever the wind blows', answered the other.

This again nonplussed the youngster, who took his defeat to his teacher.

'Ask him where is he going if there is no wind? suggested the teacher.

The next day the children meet a third time.

'Where are you going?' asked the first child.

'I am going to market to buy vegetables', the other replied.

Moral - By the time you have the answers, life changes the questions.

The 360° Mind

"A says he is not afraid. B says he is not afraid and that he is not afraid of being afraid. The 1st mind is 180° and the second mind is 360°. The 360° mind does not have any pre conceived notions - not even the pre conceived notion that there should not be any pre conceived notions. The 360° mind is open, flexible and uncontrived."

The Most Important Teaching

A renowned Zen master said that his greatest teaching was this - 'Buddha is your own mind'. So, impressed by how profound this idea was, one monk decided to leave the monastery and retreat to the wilderness to meditate on this insight. There he spent twenty years as a hermit probing this great teaching. One day he met another traveling monk in the wilderness. On learning that he had studied under the same Zen master his eyes lit up. He asked, 'please tell me of the master's greatest teaching'.

The traveling monk replied - 'Buddha is not your own mind and about this the master is very clear'.

Joshu Washes the Bowl

A monk told Joshu: 'I have just entered the monastery. Please teach me'.
Joshu asked: 'Have you eaten your rice porridge?'
The monk replied: 'I have eaten'.
Joshu said: 'Then you had better wash your bowl'.
At that moment the monk was enlightened.

Bodhidharma Pacifies the Mind

Bodhidharma sits facing the wall. His future successor stands in the snow and presents his severed arm to Bodhidharma. He cries: 'My mind is not pacified, pacify my mind'.

Bodhidharma says: 'If you bring me that mind, I will pacify it for you'.

The successor says: 'When I search my mind, I cannot hold it'.

Bodhidharma says: 'Then your mind is pacified already'.

Mind – A Monarch

Observe the empty monarch Mind; mysterious, subtle, unfathomable, it has no shape or form, yet it has great spiritual power, it is able to extinguish a thousand troubles and perfect ten thousand virtues. Although in its essence it is empty, it can provide guidance. When you look at it, it has no form; call it, and it has a voice. It acts as a great spiritual leader; mental discipline transmits scripture.

Like salt in water, like adhesive in colouring, it is certainly there, but you con't see its form; such is the monarch Mind - dwelling inside the body, going in and out of the senses, it responds freely to all beings according to conditions, without hindrance, succeeding at all it does.

When you realize the fundamental, you perceive the mind; when you perceive the mind, you see Buddha. This mind is Buddha; the Buddha is mind. Be mindful of the Buddha mind, the Buddha mind is mindful of Buddha. If you want to realize early attainment, discipline your mind, regulate yourself. When you purify your habits and purify your mind, the mind itself is Buddha; there is no Buddha other than this monarch Mind.

If you want to attain Buddhahood, don't be stained by anything. Though mind in essence is empty, the substance of greed and anger is solid. To enter this door sit straight and be Buddha. Once you've arrived at the other shore, you will attain the perfection.

To seek the way, observe your own mind yourself. When you know that Buddha is within, and do not seek it outside, then mind itself is Buddha, and Buddha is the mind. When the mind is clear, you perceive Buddha and understand the perceiving mind. Apart from mind there is no Buddha; apart from Buddha is no mind. If not for Buddha, nothing is fathomed; there is no competence at all.

If you cling to emptiness and linger in quiescence, you will bob and sink herein: the Buddhas and bodhisattvas do not rest their minds this way. Great people who clarify the mind understand this mystic message; body and mind are naturally sublimated, their action is unchanging. Therefore the wise realise that the mind is independent and free.

Do not say the monarch mind is empty in having no essential nature; it can cause the physical body to do wrong or right. Neither being nor nonbeing, it is concealed and revealed without fixation. Although in essence mind is empty, it can be ordinary or saintly: therefore I urge you to guard it carefully - a moment of contrivance, and you go back to bobbing and sinking.

The knowledge of the pure and clean mind is as yellow gold to the world; the spiritual treasury of wisdom is all in the body and mind. The uncreated spiritual treasure is neither shallow nor deep. The Buddhas and bodhisattvas understand this basic mind; for those who have the chance to encounter it, it is not past, future, or present.

Fu Shan-hui (487-569)

Mystic Understanding

Mystic understanding of truth is not perception or cognition. That is why it is said that you arrive at the original source by stopping the mind, so it is called the enlightened state of being as is, the ultimately independent free individual.

Nan-ch'uan (748-834)

Absolute Truth

The body of truth is not constructed; it does not fall into any category. Truth is unshakable; it does not depend on the objects of the six senses. Therefore, scripture says that Buddha nature is constant, while mind is inconstant. That is the sense in which knowledge is not the way and mind is not Buddha.

Therefore, do not say mind is Buddha and do not understand it in terms of perception and cognition. This thing originally does not have all those names.

Nan-ch'uan

Truth and Words

There is originally no word for truth, but the way to it is revealed by words. The way originally has no explanation, but reality is made clear by explanation. That is why the Buddhas appeared in the world with many expedient methods; the whole canon dispenses medicines according to diseases.

Shih-shuang (986-1039)

Life and Death

The matter of life and death is important; impermanence is swift. Aspirants of Zen all understand the path, but when you ask them why we live and why we die, ten out of ten are dumbstruck. If you go on this way, even if you journey throughout the whole world, what will it accomplish? Nothing.

Tuan-ch'iao

3. Wisdom in Chapter – IV

(1) Our senses provide us with an edited version of reality so do not trust reason or logic.
(2) Everything is temporary in this Universe.
(3) Live in the present.
(4) Focus, patience and perseverance are important.
(5) Your essential nature is pure.
(6) By the time you have the answers, life changes the questions.
(7) Have an open mind.
(8) Evolution is a continuous process.
(9) Enlightenment is not found outside day to day life.
(10) Aspirants understand the path, but when you ask them why we live and why we die, all are dumb struck.

Quotes

Born again? No, I'm not. Excuse me for getting it right the first time.

- Dennis Miller

I never knew how to worship until I knew how to love.

- Henry Ward Beecher

Life's Eternal Questions

What I learnt from my interactions with swamiji.

Swamji does not believe in giving discourses or in traditional teachings. You are expected to stay at the ashram with the master and discover for yourself through your own experiences. The emphasis is on experiential learning. If the sadhak has dedication it is the master's job to provide the inspiration and lead the sadhak on the path of self discovery. I have tried to intellectually pen down some of the things I have learnt from my interactions with Swamiji, but in truth my words will convey only part of the meaning. All that I have learnt from my visits to the ashram can be understood by those who have also experienced.

1. **Empty your cup (have an open mind)**

    I had gone to the sadhana kendra ashram for the first time with my family, primarily with the intention to seek blessings for my son Gaurav. Both me and my wife used to do japa but we knew very little about spirituality. In our first meeting with Swamiji, I enquired about the procedure followed by him for giving initiation. He replied that he gave the Guru mantra to anyone who brought him 'Om' written twelve lac times and that earlier he used to give the Guru mantra to anyone who wrote 'Om' 2.5 lac times. I immediately asked him whether I could write 'Ram' instead of 'Om' and he replied he was ok with it.

    I enquired about how meditation is done and he explained that the mind must be empty of all thoughts. I immediately thought this was absurd. How can the mind be empty of all thoughts?

    On reflection, it was obvious to me that my previous knowledge had been a hindrance. Had I emptied my mind of past knowledge and old habits, I would have been more open to new learning. We never realize how we approach a situation with a closed mind and limit our options. When the cup is already full, what can the master teach?

It is always wise to approach a master without any preconceived notion and without the baggage of knowledge. As the Shiva Sutras says, 'Gyanaam Bandhanam' knowledge is a bondage. If you have already formed a view on a matter, how can you be open to other ideas? Open the door of your mind, clean out the garbage and create space for new ideas and thoughts to filter in.

2. **Take a meaningful break**

   Swamiji takes a meaningful break every year for two months and spends this time in total seclusion in a cave in Jammu. Also every Monday he is in total seclusion. It is necessary that we take a meaningful pause in our lives as this will help us assess, adjust and take appropriate action as per the demands of the situation. Most of us go through life without pausing or contemplating as if this is all that life has to offer. Reflection and contemplation must be a part of our everyday life if we hope to evolve into better human beings.

3. **Enjoy the moment**

   Even though swamji is in total silence, he is laughing all the time and is in a joyful mood. This is so because swamji has decided to be happy. Happiness is a state of mind and has nothing to do with the external world. External situations are not under your control but how you will respond is within your control. Whether you let your mind be disturbed by negative emotions or not is within your control.

4. **Tightening the mind**

   Swamiji believes in concentrating all the energy of the body and mind on one specific target or goal at a time. The mind is tightened to exclude all extraneous thoughts—thoughts that are not concerned with achieving your immediate goal. He takes things as they come, so he manages to live in the present undisturbed by the past or worries about the future.

5. **Perseverance**

    Swamiji started meditating very early in his life. Even today at this old age, he spends four hours daily in group meditations at the ashram. Perseverance is the key to swamijis success. One must convince the mind that it is enjoying itself.

6. **Silence speaks**

    Swamiji writes the answers to all the questions of his disciples as he observes complete silence. In some cases he may not reply and remains silent. He remains silent when he feels that the aspirant may get his answers from the Guru within. These disciples sit with the Guru in silence and have the answers to their question answered in silence. This sounds absurd. How can you have your questions answered in silence? I have, on a few occasions, sent questions to Guruji and Swamiji has not replied but I found the answers later on in meditation. So I can vouch for the fact that it is possible for a Guru to put you in touch with the Guru within who alone will answer all your questions.

7. **Discipline and punctuality**

    The sadhana kendra ashram is run like the ashrams which existed in India in the olden days. The rules of the ashram are clearly written on a notice board and have never been changed since the ashram was set up. The timings of the four one hour long meditation sessions, and the question – answer session with Swamiji are fixed. This ashram is appropriate for the disciplined serious seeker and not appropriate for casual sight seeing. The method of meditation is not taught at this ashram although questions regarding meditation are answered by Swamiji. It is understood that you have already got basic knowledge of meditation and have come to practice at the ashram or you want to be besides the master for some time to gain inspiration to work harder on your practises. Seekers from all religions come to the ashram, there is no temple at the ashram, and it has only one sound proof meditation room for group meditation.

You are expected to arrive at the meditation hall ten minutes before the start of the meditation session and complete your preliminary formalities (body stretching, making the breath even, etc.) so that you do not disturb the other sadhaks. Swamiji leads all the four daily meditation sessions personally and always arrives at the meditation hall dot on time. The same can be said about the question answer sessions, they start dot on time and end on time. An important lesson learnt at the ashram is punctuality. You have to respect your own time and the time of others. Swamiji has spoken (in writing) about discipline several times but the spoken word does not have as much effect as experience. A short stay at the ashram definitely helps in ingraining discipline in our lives.

8. Equal to all

The ashram is open to everyone who wants to benefit from it. There are people from all religions, all nationalities and all walks of life who choose to come and stay here for short durations to transform their lives. Swamiji gives personal appointments to everyone, rich or poor, beginner or adept. He does not differentiate in any way between seekers and it is this philosophy which is reflected clearly at the ashram. All the rooms and accommodation facilities at the ashram are almost the same, there are no VIP rooms, also meals are served to all at the same time with the same facilities, and usually Guruji also helps in serving the meals.

In this Chapter I have posed Swamiji with the questions which philosophers have debated for centuries. Swamiji has given brief and pointed answers to all the questions. This is deliberate; as the intention is that the reader should not get caught up with the words but can reach the heart of truth.

The questions and replies of respected sage Chandraswami Udasin are as follows:

1. **Who am I? Your view on the same.**

Ans. A common person feels himself/herself as the physical body.

2. **What is your concept of God?**

Ans. God is omnipresent, omniscient and omnipotent and is the controller and creator of this Universe.

3. **What is the purpose of life?**

Ans. The true purpose of human life is to know directly and first hand, 'who am I?'

4. **Do you believe in reincarnation?**

Ans. Yes, I believe in the life after death. It is the soul that survives after death and takes a new birth according to its karmas.

5. **What is your moral code in relation to right and wrong?**

Ans. The moral code of right and wrong is not absolute. It changes according to the circumstances as well as the personality of a person.

6. **What has life taught you so far?**

Ans. Life has taught me that nothing, no situation, no relationship is permanent and perfect in this temporal world.

7. **Do you believe in free choice?**

Ans. The choice of a person is relatively free.

8. **Do you believe in destiny?**

Ans. Yes, I believe in destiny, but also in purusharth or self-effort.

9. **What is your concept of evolution?**

Ans. Evolution is the growth of a person at the physical, mental and spiritual level.

1. Write down your reflections on Swamiji answers.

Quotes of Albert Einstein

"Reality is merely an illusion, albeit a very persistent one"

"Only 2 things are infinity, the universe and human stupidity, and I'm not sure about the former"

"Science without religion is lame

Religion without science is blind".

"Morality is of the highest importance but for us, not for God".

Mã

Main pagal hoon mere pagalpan ki
Koi seema hi nahi
Tere pyar mein dooba hoon
Jiski koi intaha hi nahi

Yeh pyar kya hai, zarur poochenge log
Yeh kab kahan ātā hai, zarur poochenge log

Yeh woh chubhan hai jo tujhe
Lag gai thi kabhi
Jise yeh lag jai usase se door
Hota hi nahin.

I'm mad. Thare is no end to my madness.
I'm absorbed in you, unfathomable love.

The people will ask, what this love is?
They will want to know, when and where does it come?

This is the pinch that was once felt by you;
He who feels this pinch won't go away from you.

The Seeker

There is no one who does not seek,
The seeker is he who knows he seeks,
The names, forms and objects may vary,
It is the same substance we all seek,
Salutations to the One we all seek,
And the eternal game of hide and seek.
The game is 'one-sided', where can He hide?

He is the one in everything.
On the way of your search you may soon find,
Shadows and footprints of sages, sublime.
At this point my friend, Awaken and find
The earth and heavens beckon you to shine.
A seeker is one who knows he seeks
In this eternal game of hide and seek.

The Guru

In your vocabulary you may not find
A word more sacred.
In your bonds you may not find
A bond more unbreakable.
In the universe you may not find
Love more unshakeable.
When times turn bad and the world deserts you,
You may not find
A support more sustainable.
In your search you may not find
A light more reliable.
Among your friends you may not find
A friend more trustable.
To have your Guru's blessings you must walk through the gate,
You can start anytime it's never too late.
The Guru is waiting and will always wait
For you to take the bait.
When you would want what only he can give,
You have walked through the gateless gate.

Bhagwãn

Tere bãre mein main kabhi Likhtã hi nahi
I never write about you.

Aisi jurat to main kabhi kartã hi nahi
I never ever try to write.

Tere kadmon mein merã sar ho
I bow head at your feet,
Terã har hukum sar ankhon pe
I will obey all your orders.
Marte hai log main kabhi marta hi nahin
Others die, I never die.

Main hun, Tu hai yahan koi doosrã hi nahi
Only you and I are there and none else;

Tu hi tu hai yahan koi doosrã bhi nahi
Only you are everywhere and none else;

Uske kehne par main likhtã hoon warnã main likhtã hi nahin
I write when he orders, Otherwise I don't write.

Woh hai yeh sach hai
If it is true that he is,
To main hoon ke nahi
Then am I there or not?
Main hoon yeh sach hai
If it is true that I am
To woh hai ke nahi
Then is he there or not?
Sach kya hai main to janta hi nahi
What is the truth, I don't know;

Sach ek ehsãs hai lafzon mein bayan hota hi nahin
Truth is such a realisation that it cannot be expressed in words.

Quotes

"Do the difficult things while they are easy and do the great things while they are small. A journey of a thousand miles must begin with a single step".

— *Lao Tzu*

"Empty handed I entered the world, barefoot I leave it. My coming, my going; .....two simple happenings that got entangled."

— *Kozan Ichikyo*

"Ãnanda Lahari"

"Wave of bliss"
It contains forty-one stotras
In praise of Divine Mother
It also contains a series of mantras
which a seeker chants
To be used by the aspirant,
along with yantra corresponding,
wherein the *Devi* is conceived
as abiding.

Tu hi tu hai chãrsu
Hawã bhi tu
Ghatã bhi Tu
Hai meri itni ãrzoo
Rahun tere kadmon ke rubaroo.

You are everything from air to cloud;
It's my only wish to be always at your feet.

Introduction

To understand the essence of Anand Lahari several concepts of Sage Adi Shankaracharya must be understood.

1. **Concept of God :**

    Only Mother exists as Absolute Reality. It is with her power that Shiva exists as the inner dweller in every living being. The universe is created, sustained and destroyed for her pleasure and everything moves in accordance to the wishes of the Divine Mother.

It is only the virtuous and pure hearted who have direct access to Mother.

2. Concept of Worship:

There are infinite ways to worship the Mother and She accepts them all. Some methods of worship have been enumerated in the forty-one stotras.

3. Who can worship the Mother?

Only the pious and pure can worship the Mother. People who worship the Mother are never ordinary because nothing associated with Mother is ever ordinary.

The devotees of the Divine Mother gain immeasurable power and glory in the Universe.

Even on attainment of perfection, happiness may elude you if you do not have Mother's grace.

Mantra 1

Text:
Shivah shaktyã yukto yadi bhavati shaktah prabhitum;
Na chedevam devo na khalu kushalah spanditum-api
Atah-tvãm-ārādhyām hari-hara-viranchjãdi-bhih-api;
Pranantum stotum nã kathamakrit-punyah prabhavati.

Translation
Only when Shivã and Shakti are united, then Shakti becomes powerful. Thus it is true that in her absence Shiva will have no power even to move. She is worshipped by Vishnu, Shiva and Brahmã and hence only she is worth worshipping. How can one get the virtues to worship you?

Essence:
Oh divine Mother!
I bow before you
Only the virtuous can praise you,
the Demi-gods worship you
Mother! Only you have absolute existence.
Everyone else has relative existence.
Even the powerful Shiva has power only when he is
united with you.

Mantra 2

Text:
Taneeyānsu pānshu tava charana-panke-ruha-bhavam;
Viranchih sanchinvan viracvhayati lokānavikalam.
Vahatyenam shaurih kathamapi sahasrona shrasām;
Harah sankshu bhyainam bhajati bhasitoddhulan-
vidhim.

Translation
From the minutest atomic dust from your lotus feet, the cosmos is created. This is held together and moves with your power and rotates around the Sun. Because of you the creation becomes easier for Shiva, who bears it on his infinitely powerful head, and ends it by converting it into ashes.

Essence:

Oh divine Mother!
I bow to you.
It is for your pleasure
that the world is
created, sustained and destroyed.

Mantra – 3

Text:
Avidyā-nām-antasti-mira-mihir-dveep-nagari.
Jadānām chaitanya-stavaka-makarandah-trutijhari.
Daridrānām chintāmani gunanikā janma-jaladhau.
Nimagnānām danshtrā muraripurāhasya bhavati.

Translation:
O Mother! You are like a lighted island in the dark ocean of ignorance; you give light like numerous Suns; you are the light of knowledge to the living beings surrounded by darkness. You are like a fountain of juice in the desert like space. It is because of your kindness that in a dried up life, one feels cosy shade. You free the living beings as Vishnu freed the earth in the form of Vārāha.

Essence:
Oh Divine Mother!
I bow before you.
You are the bestower of grace,
you can give knowledge
to the ignorant.
life to the lifeless,
wealth to the poor.
It is your grace that can lead one
to the other shore.

Mantra-4

Text:
Jvad-anyah pānibhyām bhaya-vardo daivta-gana.
Stavam-yekāmaivāsi prokatita-varā-bhitya-abhinayā.
Bhayāt-trātum datum phalam-api cha vānchhā-
samadhikam;
Sharanye lokānām tava hi charanāveva nipunau.

Translation
The whole Universe is created with the dust and movement of your feet and from which all the God-heads have appeared. You save all from fear and grant more than asked for. All God forms with their hands show gesture of protection and granting wishes. You alone are not seen that way. What is the need when you protect and give more than desired?

Essence:

Oh Divine Mother!
I bow before you
You are the true
protector and giver.
Everyone comes to you
for protection
and you do the needful,
giving people more than
they deserve.

Mantra-5

Text:
Harih-tvām ārādhya pranat-jane-saubhāgya-jananeem;
Purā nāri bhutvāpura-ripum-api kshobham-anayat.
Smaro-api tvām natvā rati-nayan-le hyena vapushā;
Muninām-apyantah prabhavati hi mohāya mahatma.

Translation:
O Mother of all! You grant all fortunes to them who worship you. By worshipping you, Vishnu turned into a woman and enchanted even Shiva. Kāmadeva, with the physical beauty admired by the eyes of Rati, creates lascivous desires in the hearts of learned sages also.

Essence:
Oh Divine Mother!
There is nothing you cannot do.
You grant fortune to those who worship you.
Blessed are those who worship you.
The universe spins on your little finger
and even the learned ones
can succumb to desire
when faced with it. Fortunate
are the ones who worship you.

Mantra-6

Text:
Dhanuh panshpam maurvi madhukar-mayi pancha-vishikhãh;
Vasantah samanto Malaya-maruda-ayodhan-rathah.
Tathã-pyckah sarvam himgiri-sute kãm-api kripãm;
Apãngata te labdhatã jagadi-damango vijayate.

Translation:
Born in the Himalayas, Kãmadeva, the god of sex, all alone with only five arrows, and bow of nothing but flowers and the bow-string of restless and ever buzzing bees; he on the chariot of mountain breeze with his minister Spring which comes for a short time once in a year, has conquered the whole world and is declared victorious only because of the mercy of the slightest glance of your beautiful eyes.

Essence:
Oh Divine Mother!
I bow before you.
Even the weakest would win
if your mercy is received,
Even through a sideward glance
if you bestow your grace,
victory over the universe is assured.

Mantra-7

Text:
Kvanat-kãnchi dãmã kari-kalabha-kumbha-stana-natã;
Parikheenãmadhye parinat-sharat-chandra-vadanã.
Dhanuh-vãnãn-pãsham srinim-api dadhãnã kar-talaih;
Purastãdãstãm nah puram-athi-tuvãho-punishikã.

Translation:
Thin of waist but heavy of bosom, slightly bent with jingling chains around your waist, you possess a face with the beauty of the full moon of winter season; carrying in your hands your bow, arrow, rope and sickle; you give the sense of individuality to Shiva who destroys all the world.

Essence:

Oh Divine Mother!
My senses and mind exist
because you have given Shiva the
power
of manifesting as the inner light
in all creatures,
and yet you are not different from Shiva;
In truth only you exist.

Mantra-8

Text:
Sudhā-sindhuh-madhye sur-vita-pivāte-parivrite;
Mani-dripe neepa-apavan-vati chintā-mani grihe.
Shivākāre manede param-shiva-paryanka-nilayām;
Bhajanti tvām dhanyāh katichan chida-ānand-tahari.

Translation:
They are fortunate and pious people who worship you as the Ultimate Bliss by the side of Shiva on a seat of manifested goodness inside a house made up of gems in the garden of kadamba trees, in the island of jewels amidst the sea of nectar surrounded by the kalpa, the all wishes fulfilling trees.

Essence:

Oh Divine Mother!
Infinite are the
ways in which people
worship you;
you accept them all.

Mantra-9

Text:
Maheem moolãdhãre kamapi manipure luta-uaham;
Sthitam swãdhishthãne hridi manutam-ãkãsham-upari.
Mano-api bhrumadhye sakalam-api bhitvã kulapatham;
Sahasrãre padme sah rahasi patyã viharasi.

Translation:
In the Moola-ãdhãra, at the lower end of the spine, manifesting as the earth and as the water spirit in the Manipuraka chakra; as the spirit in the Swãdhistãn chakra, and in the heart; as the wind spirit; slightly above as the space spirit and as the mind spirit in between the brows, the energy is concentrated as in a yogi, which is an unknown phenomenon to the other human beings. O Mother! You manifest as the Ultimate Bliss in the thousand petalled lotus, Sahasrãr chakra breaking the doors of all these paths.

Essence :

Oh Divine Mother!
In a normal person
you are asleep,
but in a yogi
you are awake.
You provide the yogi
with ultimate bliss.

Mantra-10

Text:
>Sudhã-thãvã-saraih-charan-jugalãntah-vigalitaih;
>Praponcham sinjanti-punah-api rasãmnãya-mahasãh.
>Avãpya swam bhumi muja-ganibha-madhya-ushta-
>valayam;
>Swam-ãtmãnam kritvãswapishi kula-kundi kuharini.

Translation:
From the chakra of Sahasrãra Padma, the enlightening sphere of a thousand petalled lotus, the whole world is watered by the rasa, juice, nectar, flowing from within your feet; and then returning to your own land; making you coil like a snake in slumber at the lower end of spine as dormant Kundalini.

Essence:
>*Oh Divine Mother!*
>*The nectar of knowledge*
>*flows on your command*
>*all over the universe.*
>*People do not know*
>*about your power,*
>*as you lie as if in a slumber*
>*as the unaroused*
>*Kundalini.*

Mantra-11

Text:
Chaturblik shri-kanthaik shiva-yuvati-bhih panch-bhih-api;
Prabhin-nābhih shambhoh-nava-bhih-api moola-prakriti-bhih.
Trayah-chatvārim-shadva-sudal-kalābja-trivalaya;
Tri-rekhābhih sardham tava charana konāh parinatāh.

Translation:
The nine chakras—four belonging to Shiva and five to others, are different from Shiva Chakras. They are related to the basic nature of the Universe, Moola Prakiti. They have converted your Shree Chakra into forty four angles along with an eight petalled lotus, a sixteen petalled lotus like the kalā phases of Moon with three circles and three lines.

Essence:
Oh Divine Mother!
Among the many types of
worship, you are also worshipped
Through Shree Chakras .

Mantra-12

Text:
Tvadeeyam saundaryam tuhin-giri-kanye tulayitum;
Karindrāh kalpante kathamapi virarchi prabhritayah.
Yada lokaut-shkanad-amar-lalanā yānti manasā;
Tapo-bhih-dush-prāpām-api girish-sājujya-padavim.

Translation:
The daughter of the mighty Himalayas, the poets have failed to describe your beauty; your beauty is indescribable even for knowledgeable ones like Brahmā and others. The beautiful women of the heavens reach Shiva through great penance so that they could see your olivine force.

Essence:
Oh Divine Mother!
The universe is an expression of your
love, creativity and beauty.
It is not possible to
perceive your beauty and might
through the human mind.
Your beauty is difficult to perceive
even for heavenly creatures and they are
always eager for your sideward glance.
It is not through
Tapas or other practices that
your beauty can be perceived.
Your beauty can be perceived only
through your grace.

Mantra-13

Text:
Naram varshiyãnsam nayan-virasam narmasu jadane;
Tara-ãpãng-ãloke patitam-anudhavanti shatashah.
Gale-dveni-bandhãh kucha-kalash-visrast-sichayã;
Hathãt-trutjat-kãanchayo vigalita-dukulã yuvatayah.

Translation:
Hundreds of young women with loose hair, falling off dresses, broken chains, unveiled bosom, with determination follow an old man with faint eyes, almost lifeless and effeminate only because of your blessing with only a sideward glance.

Essence:
Oh Divine Mother!
The Universe is eager to honour
anyone favoured by your sideward
glance. It is you who assigns
worth to man.
Even an ant would be more
powerful than Indra
if it has been favoured
by your sideward glance.
It is your grace which
Makes people desirable and beautiful.

Mantra-14

Text:

Kshitau shat-panchãshat dvi-saneadhik-panchãshad-uduke;
Hutãshe dvashastih-chatur-adhik-panchãshad-anile.
Divi dvih shat-trishan-manasi cha chatuh-shashleh-iti ye;
Mayukhãh-teshãm-apyupari tava pada-ambuja-yugam.

Translation:
Your feet are above five gross elements whose centre has 360 degrees, Kalã or phases out of which 56 belongs to the earth, 52 to ocean, 62 to fire; 54 to air, 72 to space and 64 belongs to mind. Thus they possess all the powers of creation and living beings.

(This is also explained as the phases or Kalã of different chakras of Kundalini.)

Essence:
O Divine Mother!
It is an honour to enumerate your glories.
It is through your power that Shiva becomes the inner
dweller manifesting as the life force in every creature.
It is for your delight that the universe continues
in its cosmic dance.
The elements are created and sustained
from the dust at your lotus feet.
The human mind is unable to perceive your true
glory because the senses are not capable of providing
complete data about reality, but everything in the Universe
emanates from the dust at your lotus feet,
And is for your ultimate pleasure.

Mantra-15

Text:
Sharat-jyatsanā-shubhrām shashi- yuta-jatā-juta-mukutām;
Var-trāna-sphatika-ghntikā-pustak-karām.
Sakrinna tvām na tvām katha-mewa satām sannida-dhate;
Madhu-kheer-drākshā-madhuri-madhurinābhanitayah.

Translation:
You are brighter than the brightest winter-full moon; your hair is decorated with the crown of a crescent moon; your expert hands hold the rosary of quartz and a book; and are projected in the gesture of showering blessings. With pure devotion if one worships you even once, he will utter nectar like ideas in words as sweet as honey, milk and grapes.

Essence:

Oh Divine Mother!
There are infinite ways in which you are
Worshipped and infinite ways to please you as
You are not bound by any rules.
Even an uneducated man would become a poet
if he was favored by your grace.
Oh Divine Mother!
Only you can give to man
all that he desires as only
you have absolute power.

Mantra-16

Text:
Kavindrānām cheetah kamal-va-bātā-tap-ruchim;
Bhajante ye santah kati-chid-arunām-yeva bhavatim.
Varinchi-preya-syāh-taruntar-shringaār-laharim;
Gabhirābhih-vāgibhih-vidadhati satām ranjanamami.

Translation:
The minds of great poets are like lotus fields looking up to the beauty of the rising Sun. Those pious poets who worship you with a little rosy hue, entertain people who are good at heart with great words; who are filled up with youthful vigour and sweet lilting words like that of Devi Saraswati, the mother of letters and words, Varna and Shabd.

Essence:

Oh Divine Mother!
The pious and pure-hearted people
worship you in many ways.
The gifts that you grant to the
pure hearted are such that
they can perceive the beauty of the Universe,
and when they enumerate the
beauty of the Universe, it is so
fascinating that the words seem to
be those of Mother Saraswati.

Mantra-17

Text:
Sãvitrībhih-vāachām shashi-mani-sheelã-bhanga-ruchibhih;
Vashinyādyã-bhih-tvām sah janani sanchintayati yah.
Sa kartā kãvyāhm bhavati mahtām bhangi-subhageh;
Vacho-bhih-vãgdevi-vadan-kamal-ãmod-madhuraih.

Translation:
O Mother! Whoever remembers you along with your vashinyaa and other beautiful rays, composes such great epics whose words have the sweetness and glow of the moon-stone, cut and polished. He creates such beautiful poetry that possesses the greatness of great poets and the sweet musical words like the lotus face, filled up with joy of the Vãgdevi, mother of sound and words.

Essence:

Oh Divine Mother!
Oh Mother, whoever worships you
in any form is never ordinary.
People who worship you are like
diamonds who need polishing
to discover their true worth,
for nothing associated with you is ever
ordinary. With your blessings nothing is
impossible and even an ordinary man
could create poetry like that of Kalidas.
Oh Mother!
You are the bestower of beauty and bliss in the universe.

Mantra-18

Text:
> Iatu-chhãya-bhh-te tarun-larani-dri-dharani-bhih;
> Divam sarvã-murvim-aruni-mani-magnã smarati yah.
> Bhavantyasya trasya-dvan-harin-shaleena-nayanãh;
> Saha-urvashyãh kati kati na grivã-gana-ganik.

Translation:
Most beautiful heavenly nymphs like Urvasi, with beautiful eyes like that of wild deer running in fear, becomes his own, who worships your bright divine form immersed in the entire Earth and the rosy hue of the rays of the rising Sun.

Essence:

Oh Divine Mother!
You are the bestower of beauty
in the universe and beauty in
every form follows those who
worship you.
Beauty is a matter of perception,
and you are the bestower of perception
in the universe.

Mantra-19

Text:
Muklam bindu kritvã mucha-yugma-adhas-tasya taddho;
Hora-ardham dhyãyidyo har-mahishi te manmath-kalãm.
Sa sadyah sankshobham nayati vanitã iti-ati-laghu;
Trilokimap yãshu bhramayati yarindu-stan-yugãm.

Translation:
O the Queen of Shiva! He, who worship you and meditates on your face as a point, your bosom below and the half of Shiva, ardha nãrishware below, on your manmatha Kalã, immediately wins over the women. But that is nothing, he instantaneously, also wins over the entire Universe with the Sun and the Moon on its bosom.

Essence:
Oh Divine Mother!
Pious people who worship you
find that they have received
Much more than they hoped for
as there is no limit to how much you can give.
A person who worships you gains
power and influence in the Universe
and finds along with his physical desires all other desires
also fulfilled.
Oh Mother!
It is my good luck that I have the opportunity
to chant your glories.

Mantra-20

Text:
Kiranjtim-ange-bhyah kiran-nikuru-ambām-amrit-rasam;
Hridi tvām-ādhatte himkar-sheelā-murtim-eva yah.
Sa sarpānām darpam shamayati shakunta-ādhip eva;
Jvar-plustān-drishtayā sukhayati sudhā-sār-sirayā.

Translation:
The seeker, who worship your white and bright moon-stone like face from which the nectar like rays come out, wins over the arrogance of the king of snakes as if he is garuda, the king of birds. The one in great pain with fever is immediately cured by a simple glance.

Essence:

Oh Divine Mother!
Your devotees have the power to humble
even the most powerful beings in the universe.
With your grace your devotees
enjoy immense power and influence
in the Universe.
It is only the lucky ones who get a chance to
love you and worship you
because only you can turn around the universe
for love.

Mantra-21

Text:
Tadit-lekhā-tanvim tapana-shashi-vaishvā-nar-mayim;
Nishnnām shannām-apyupari kamalānām tava kalām.
Mahā-padma-ātvyām mridit-amalam-āyena manasā;
Mahāntah pashyanto dadhati param-ahlād-laharim.

Translation:
The seekers with great minds cleansed off all evils, when worship you and meditate on your sensuous form with the beauty of a flash of lightning, manifesting as the Sun, the Moon and the Fire, experience with their minds, the ultimate enjoyment that sets their heart rising in bliss, seeing your brilliant glow situated on the highest point Shad chakra, six lotuses in the great field of golden lotuses, Mahāpadma, the sahasrār chakra.

Essence:

Oh Divine Mother!
Only the pure hearted and pious have
access to you and know you.
These pure hearts with your blessings experience
the ultimate bliss as you are the bestower
of ultimate bliss in the Universe.

Mantra-22

Text:

Bhavãni tvam dãse mayi vitar drishtim sakarunãmiti;
Stotum vanchhan-kathayati bhavãni tvam-iti yah.
Tadaiva fvam tasmai dishasi nija-sayujya-padavim;
Mukund-brahmendra-sphuta-mukuta-nirãjita-padãam.

Translation:
Whoever willing to say this, 'O Mother Bhavãni! On me, your servant, do place your merciful gaze,' and the moment he starts to says this and is able to say only bhavãni tvam, 'O Mother! Your..... you immediately grant him a place near your feet to such a one. Your feet are so important that offerings are given by the flame like glows of the crowns of Brahmã, Vishnu and Indra.

Essence:

Oh Divine Mother!
You are the great one with Indra ,Vishnu and Brahma
always at your feet in worship.
It is for your pleasure that the universe
exists and yet you do not allow a
devotee to humble himself
in anyway before you .
You share a bond of love with all
your devotees and treat them like your
own children.
Your devotees are always
uplifted through your grace
and can never call themselves your servants.

Mantra-23

Text:
Tvayã hritvã vãamam vapul-aparitriptena manasã;
Sharira-ardham shambhuh-aparam-api shanke hritam-bhut.
Yade-tattva-adrupam sakalam-arunãbham trinayanam;
Kuchãbhyãm-ãnambram kutila-shashi-chudãla mukutam.

Translation:
Your form in any mind is holy with a red glow, with three eyes, bent forward because of the weight of your bosom, and a crown decorated with a crescent moon. Therefore, it seems to me, that dissatisfied even after stealing the left half of Shiva's body, you have also stolen the other half.

(When Shiva tattva gets mixed with Shakti tattva, then the latter prevails.)

Essence:

Oh Divine Mother!
The entire Universe is in a cosmic dance to
please you, it is with your power that Shiva becomes
the inner dweller in every living being .
People aiming for perfection try to be like Shiva.
But even with perfection one will not be happy
if he does not have your grace.
You are the embodiment of love and compassion,
and without these virtues, the human mind is incomplete
and perfection has no value.

Mantra-24

Text:

Tagat-sute dhātā harit-avati rudah kshapayate;
Tiras-kurvanne-tatswan-api vapuri-shastih-yati.
Sadā-pwrvah sarvam tadidam-anugrihnāti cha;
Shiva-stva-āgyām-alambya kshar-chalitayoh-blru-catikayoh.

Translation:

Brahmā creates the world, Vishnu sustains it and Rudra destroys it. The Absolute God, Ishwar, destroys all and reduces everything into nothingness including his own self. Then the bliss spoken of as 'Eternal' resets them depending on the directions given by the momentary movement of your eye-brows. Because of your indication, Shiva saves it in seed form, and with it creates the Universe again.

Essence:

Oh Divine Mother!
The world is created sustained and destroyed
for your pleasure.
There is nothing Brahma, Vishnu and Rudra
would not do to please you.
Everything in the Universe moves as per your
wishes as you are the only absolute reality.

Mantra-25

Text:
Jrayānām devānām triguna-janitānām tava Shiva;
Bhavet pooja tava charanayoh-yām virachitā.
Tathāhi tvat-pād-udvahana-mani-peethasya nikate;
Stthā hyete shaswan-nukulit-kara-utansa-mukutāh.

Translation:
O Mother Shive! Whatever poojā, worshipping is done at your feet, also becomes the pooja of the trinity of Brahmā, Vishnu and Mahesh, who are born of your three qualities, sattva, rajas and tamas, as they are present at your footrest with folded hands in your respect with their shining crowns.

Essence:
Oh Divine Mother!
I am honoured to chant your glories.
Once a devotee worships you,
he need not go anywhere else because
the entire Universe is at your feet.
You are the only one worshipable
and only the pure hearted
have access to you.

Mantra-26

Text:
Viranelih panchatvam brajati harih-āmoti viratim;
Vināsham keenāsho bhajati dhando yati nidhanam.
Vitandri māhendri vitatih-api sammilati drishām;
Mahā-sanhare-asmio-viharati sati tvat-patih-asau.

Translation:
The purest Brahmā is reduced to nothing; Vishnu reaches the end of his existence; Death itself is destroyed; Kubera gets mitigated; the Manus also close their eyes and become lifeless. At that time of total destruction, only your spouse Shiva happily moves in the worlds.

Essence:

Oh Divine Mother!
When the entire universe comes to an end,
you are the only one that remains,
as you are without a beginning or end.
You are the only Absolute reality
and bliss is your essential nature.

Mantra-27

Text:

Japo jalpah shilpam sakalam-api mudrã-virachanam;
Gatih prãdakshinyam kramanam-shanãdya-ãhuti-vidhih.
Pranãmah samveshah sukham-akhilam-ãtma-arpan-dashã;
Lapãrya-apãrja-ãyastva bhavatu janme vilasitam.

Translation:

O Mother! May everything I say be a prayer; everything I do be mudras, gestures of worship; when I walk, may it be pradakshinã, movement around you; may everything that I eat be the offer in a homa, as offering to fire during poojã; when I lie down, may it be my namaskãr, prostration before you; may every movement of mine be what you would be fond of! May it be another form of your worship in total surrender.

Essence:

Oh Divine Mother!
I wish to completely surrender to you.
May everything I do be an expression
of my love and surrender
to you.

Mantra-28

Text:

Sudhãm-ãsvãdya pratibhaya-jara-mrityu-haranim;
Vipadyante vishwe vidhi-shatam-khãdyã divi shadah.
Karãlam yatkshvelam kavalit-vatah kãla-kalanã;
Na shambhoh-tanmoolam janani tava tãtank-mahimã.

Translation:

O Mother! Brahmã, Indra and all other godheads ultimately meet an end even after drinking the nectar of everlasting life and youth which destroys old age and the ferocious death. However, your spouse Shiva, who took the most terrible of poisons, meets no such end because of the quality and effect of your ear-studs, (which can be woven only by the purest one, and which did not allow the poison to go down the throat.)

Essence:

Oh Divine Mother!
What would one do with eternal life if one is not happy?
With your grace a curse can become a blessing, for
you are the bestower of ultimate bliss.
Eternal life is not worth
having if your grace is missing.

Mantra-29

Text:
Kiritam vairichyam pari harpurah kaitabhabhidah;
Kathore koteere skhalase jahi jambhāri mukutam.
Pranamreshveteshu prasabham-upayā-tasya bhavanam;
Bhavasyā-abhyutthāne tava parijanoktih-vijayate.

Translation:
As you got up from your seat to welcome your spouse Shiva on his sudden entry into your palace, the maids at your service warned you to move away from Brahma's crown; to avoid slipping against the very hard crown of Vishnu and to leave the crown of Indra because they all worship at your feet.

Essence:

Oh Divine Mother!
Indra, Brahma and Vishnu are at your feet
always finding ways to please you.
They have the universe
at their command
and yet you are not bothered about them.
And when Shiva who has nothing but love for you
needs you, you are concerned.
You have given Indra, Brahma and Vishnu
the Universe, and Shiva your love
and respect.
You alone can bestow worth to your devotees.

Mantra-30

Text:
*Swa-deha-udbhootā-abhih-ghrinibhih-animā-ākshyā-abhih-mito;
Nishevye nitye tvām-ahmiti sadā bhāvayati yah.
Kim-āshcharejam lasya trinayan-smriddhim trinayato;
Mahā-samvartā-agrih-virachayati nirājan-vidhim.*

Translation:
O Eternal Mother! You are served and surrounded by Ashta-siddhis (Animā etc). The great seeker who worships your feet after complete surrender, and always thinks only of you, feels the post of Indra to be a straw. The flames of the all devouring fire at the time of total destruction are powerless before your devotee.

Essence:
*Oh Divine Mother!
All life springs from your grace.
There is nothing greater than to see you in myself.
It is with your power that Shiva is the inner dweller
in every
living being. Wherever I see love, I get
a glimpse of your true self.*

Mantra-31

Text:
Chatuh-shashtayā tantraih sakalam-iti-sandhāya bhauanam;
Sthita-tata-siddhi-prasara-par-tatraih pashupatim.
Punah-tvanrih-bandhāt-akhil-purushārthaik-ghatanā;
Swatantram te tantram kshiti-talam-avāti-tar-didam.

Translation:
The master of all the worlds, Shiva revealed Sixty four Tantra-Shāstras to the world creating an illusion by their separate and different gains, but later on, under your compulsion, manifested this technique of yours on the earth which is capable of independently granting every desire.

Essence:

Oh Divine Mother!
The impure devotees do not manage to
access you directly
but have their desire fulfilled,
and some of them can do super normal feats,
but your pure devotees access you
directly and gain the ultimate bliss.

Mantra-32

Text:
Shivah shaktih kãnah kshitirath rabih sheeta-kiran;
Smaro hansah shakrah-tadance cha parāmār-harajah.
Ami hrillekhã-abhisti-sribhih-vasāneshu ghatitā;
Bhajante varnāste tava janani nāmā-vayavatām.

Translation:
O Mother! There are your three Kuta Mantras-
1. K A E L Hring which means K Shiva; A Shakti; E Kãm; L earth and Hring Hrillokhã.
2. H S K H L Hring representing H Rivah; S Soma; K Smarah; H Hansah; L Shakra and Hring Hrillokhã.
3. S K L Hring symbolizing S Parã Shakti; K Mãrah; L Hari and Hring Hrillokhã.

By chanting them a seeker is freed from every obstacle.

Essence:
Oh Divine Mother!
The Shree Vidya Mantra is used to gain access
to you for you are the ultimate fulfiller of desires.
In truth there are infinite ways to worship
you and only you know what pleases you.
Words of a Mantra are useless unless they are said
with love and devotion.
You are aware of the heartbeat of every living creature and Only
you know the truth about the motivation of your devotees.
It is my honour to enumerate your glories.

Mantra-33

Text:
Smaram yonim laxamim tri-tayam-idam-ādau tava;
Manoh-nidhāyaike nitye niravadhi-mahā-bhoga-rasikāh.
Bhajanti tvām chintamani-guna-nibaddhāksha-valayah;
Shivāgram juhvantah surabhi-ghrita-dhārā-āhuti-shataih.

Translation:
O Mother Eternal! With a desire to get all the luxuries of life, some seekers worship you and meditate wearing garlands dense with divine precious stones with the three beeja mantras; Kling, Kāma Beeja Mantra; hring, Yoni Beeja Mantra and Shri, Luxmi Beeja Mantra at the beginning (centre) of your Pancha-dasha-akshari-mantra; and offer into the fire, flow of ghee of the heavenly cow Kāmadhenu. They enjoy limitless bliss.

Essence:

Oh Divine Mother!
Some devotees do puja
with elaborate rituals, and
some do it only through the mind.
Puja done using the mind is enjoyable and effective.

Mantra-34

Text:
Shariram tvam shambhoh shashi-mihir-vakcha-uruh-yugam;
Tava-ātmānam manye bhagavati bhava-ātmānam-anagham.
Atah sheshah sheshitya-yam-ubhaya-sādhārantayā;
Sthitah sambandho vām sama-rasa-par-ānand-parayoh.

Translation:
O Mother Bhagavati! You are the form of Shiva himself. With the Sun and the Moon on your bosom. I know your form to be the great and unstained form of Shiva as Ānand Bhairava. Therefore, Devi and Deva become one and common to you as both are one and the same: Ultimate Bliss beyond everything.

Essence:

Oh Divine Mother!
You are the only absolute reality.
You are the only bestower of bliss
which transcends everything.
You are what we address as Shiva
and
yet Shiva has relative reality
and
you are the only absolute reality.

Mantra-35

Text:

Manastvam vyom tvam marud-asi marut-sãrathih-asi;
Tvam-ãpah tvam bhumih tva-api parinatãyãm nahi param.
Tvam-yeva swa-ãtmãnam parinamayifum vishwa-vapushã;
Chid-ãnand-ãkãram shiva-yuvati bhãvena vibhrishe.

Translation:
O Mother! You are the Mind; You are the Space; You are the Air; You are the Fire; You are the Water; You are the earth; There is nothing which is not of you or not from you. As the manifestation of the Universe, and as the spouse of Shiva, you are the Ultimate Inner Bliss.

Essence:

Oh Divine Mother!
It is for your pleasure
that the Universe has been created,
there is nothing apart from you.
You are the giver of life,
yet O Mother,
few see you as you are.

Mantra-36

Text:
Tava-ãgyã-chakrastham tapan-shashi-koti-dyuti-dharam;
Param shambhum vande pari-milita-pãrshvam parachitã.
Yama-ãrãdhyan-bhaktyã ravi-shashi shuche-nãm-vishaye;
Virãtanke loko nivasati he bhãloka-bhavane.

Translation:
O Mother! I bow before Shiva, the Ultimate Bliss joined with you by your side in the ãgyã chakra with the luminescence of a million Suns and Moons worshipping with great devotion. The devotee lives in the world influenced by neither the Sun nor the Moon, nor Fire. He lives in the unseen world which is filled up with only the Absolute Light.

Essence:

Oh Divine Mother!
The yogi who worships Shiva,
your consort, with great devotion,
lives in a world
of absolute bliss.
Such a yogi can create
anything he wants for himself,
for everything in the universe is created by your grace.
Oh Mother! You take great care
of your devotees.

Mantra-37

Text:
Vishuddhau te shuddha sphatika vishadam vyom-janakam;
Shivam seve devion-api Shiva-samãn-vyavasitãm.
Yayoh kãntyã shashi-kiran-sãrupya-saranim;
Vidhutãnt adharvãntã vilasati chakoriva jagati.

Translation:
O Mother! In your crystal clear Vishuddhi Chakra, I worship Shiva, the eternal bliss from whom the space spirit is born. I also worship you, Mother! The equal of Shiva by the beautiful glow of both, through which the whole world becomes free from the inner darkness, and dense ignorance of the self. Then in the glow of the moonlight it dances like Chakori (She-partridge) that can drink the moonlight.

Essence:

Oh Divine Mother!
Your devotee is bathed
in the light of bliss which only your grace can provide.
I worship you as Shiva and Shakti,
and thereby I am free from the shackles of ignorance
and bathe in the light of knowledge and wisdom.

Mantra-38

Text:

Sam-unmital-sanvit-kamal-makarandaik-rasikam;
Bhaje hansa-dvandvam kimoapi mahatma mãnas-charam.
Yada-ãlãp-pãde-ashtã-dashe-gunita-vidye-parinatih;
Yada-ãdatte doshãd yunam-akhilam-adbhyah pai eva.

Translation:
O Mother Energy! I worship the inexplicable twin swans which live in the minds of great men and enjoy only the inner knowledge like the nectar inside the fully bloomed lotus. The eighteen qualities, 10 Mahãvidyãs and Shaktis, are born from it. These swans are capable of distinguishing good and healthy from bad and unhealthy as they easily separate milk from water.

Essence:

Oh Divine Mother!
I bow before the pure yogis who worship you
for it is only they who enjoy inner knowledge
and can distinguish between good and evil.

Mantra-39

Text:
Tawa swadhishthane huta-vaham-adhichthãya niratam;
Tameede samvartam janani mahatim tãm cha samayãm.
Yad-ãlike lokãn-dahati mahati krodha-kalite;
Dayãdra yad-dristtih shishiram-upachãram rachayati.

Translation:
O Mother! Placing Rudra, who ultimately destroys the Universe, in your Swãdhisdthãn chakra, so full of fire, I worship him continuously. I also worship Samaya Devi, the Goddess of Time. When those great destructive forces burn the world into ashes, then, it is your merciful glance, from the Manipuraka Chakra that cools the world like shishir, the winter Season.

Essence:

Oh Divine Mother!
Your devotees know that at the time
of destruction of the universe;
it is only your merciful glance which will save them.
It is only you who can provide ultimate protection.

Mantra-40

Text:
Taditvantam shaktyā timir-paripanthi-sphuranayā;
Sphuran-nānā-ratna-ābharan-parinadhe-indra-dhanushan.
Tava shyāman megham kamapi swādhishthān-sharanam;
Nisheve varshantam har-mihir-taptam tribhuvanani.

Translation:
O Mother! I worship the inexplicable Shiva, the Ultimate Bliss, as a black rain-cloud situated in your Manipooraka Chakra with a flash of lightning that destroys the dense darkness of ignorance by its brilliant illumination and with decoration of different gems whose glow forms the rainbow which is coiled around all the three worlds burning under the rays and heat of the Sun, Rudra.

Essence:

Oh Divine Mother!
Your grace bestows knowledge and wisdom on
your devotees;
it is with this knowledge that your devotees lose fear
and live under your protection.

Mantra-41

Text:
Tava-ãdhãre moole sah samayayã lãsya-parayã;
Nav-ãtmãnam manye nava-rasa-maha-tãndava-natam.
Ubhayã-bhyãm-yetã-bhyãm-udaya-vidhim-udrishya dayayã;
Sanãthã-bhyãm jagye janak-jananim-jagat-idam.

Translation:
O Mother! I meditate on the formless form of Shiva, in your Moolãdhãr Chakra, busy in Mahã Tandava, the great dance of Creation and Destruction with the nine expressions of art, along with Devi Samaya, the Goddess of Time. Fascinated by the dance, full of mercy and for the sake of re-creating these two forces, Shiva and Shakti have joined together. Thus this world has acquired a sense of belonging to a father and a mother.

Essence:

Oh Divine Mother!
How do I describe the cosmic dance which exists for your pleasure?
Only you know how or why the universe is created and destroyed.
I know only that I am a child, and you, my mother will protect me.

Wisdom of 'Ānanda Lahari'

To summarize the wisdom of Ananda Lahari is like trying to hold the water of an entire ocean in your palm. Each stanza of the forty-one stanzas of Ananda Lahari is said to have magical power. To those who believe in her, no explanation is necessary, to others, none would suffice.

To have the opportunity to comment on 'Ananda Lahari' is an honour beyond belief.

Let us together go forward and encounter the magic.

(1) The Divine Mother is an absolute reality and only the pure hearted and the virtuous have direct access to the Mother.

(2) There are infinite ways to worship the Mother and Mother accepts them all.

(3) The Mother is truly the 'One without a second'.

(4) The world is created, sustained and destroyed for her pleasure.

(5) The Mother is the true protector and giver. She always gives more than you deserve. To love the Mother is the primal instinct of all beings as Mother is 'life' personified.

(6) The Mother lies beyond the realm of duality and non-duality. The Universe spins on her little finger.

(7) Mother's love is unconditional and one-sided. Without her love, even a person with power and money would be miserable. Only Mother's love ensures bliss and peace of mind.

(8) You are everywhere yet you are unseen. Only you can grant true vision so that you can be seen.

(9) The Mother is compassionate and forgives easily.

(10) Beauty is a matter of perception and the Mother is the bestower of perception in this universe.

(11) All the gods are always at the Mother's feet in worship and yet she does not allow a devotee to humble himself/herself in anyway before her.

(12) Perfection has no value if Mother's grace is missing.

(13) A blessing can become a curse and a curse can become a blessing, for the mother is the bestower of ultimate bliss.

(14) Everything is not as it seems in this universe. Only the Mother knows the truth.

(15) Wherever you see love, you get a glimpse of divine Mother.

(16) Words of a mantra are useless unless said with love and devotion.

(17) Only the Mother knows what pleases her.

(18) She is Shiva and Shakti and everything that lies beyond.

(19) Only those yogis who worship the Mother in any form have true perception.

(20) At the time of death only the Mother can save her devotees.

(21) The Mother's devotees have true perception and therefore, live without fear.

(22) Only the Mother knows truly why we live and why we die. Everything is for her pleasure. I know that I am only a child and my Mother will protect me.

Glossary

Avaidika	Not as per the rules of the scared Vedas
Bija Mantra	Given by the guru as the first initiation
Bhagvad Gita	Sacred book of the Hindus
Brahman	Impersonal aspect of the Supreme Being
Chakras	Spiritual centers of energy
Guru	Teacher who dispels ignorance
Guru Mantra	Usually given by guru during the 2nd formal initiation
Japa	God remembrance
Kundalini	Primal force latent at the end of the spinal cord
Karma	Action
Maha Vidya	Great Knowledge
Mantra	Syllable or set of words revealed to sages in super consciousness
Maya	Illusion
Sadhana	Spiritual practice
Sadhak	Spiritual aspirant
Shakti Worshippers	They worship the Divine Mother
Stotras or slokas	Set of sacred words of wisdom
Samadhi	Super conscious state
Sutras	Thread joining pearls of wisdom
Siddhis	Extra-ordinary Powers
Shiva	Supreme Reality
Swamiji	Respectful address to a monk
Tantra	Philosophy aimed at experiencing non duality
Upanishad	Set of yogic and vedantic scriptures
Vedas	Sacred text of Hindus

www.ingramcontent.com/pod-product-compliance
Lightning Source LLC
Chambersburg PA
CBHW070335230426
43663CB00011B/2332